PERSPECTI
TEACHER EDUCATION REFORM
Unique Partnership Initiatives

Dr. Earline Simms

Dr. Cash J. Kowalski

Dr. Barbara J. O'Neal

South Carolina State University

McGraw-Hill Custom Publishing

Boston Burr Ridge, IL Dubuque, IA Madison, WI New York San Francisco St. Louis
Bangkok Bogotá Caracas Lisbon London Madrid
Mexico City Milan New Delhi Seoul Singapore Sydney Taipei Toronto

PERSPECTIVES IN TEACHER EDUCATION REFORM
Unique Partnership Initiatives

McGraw-Hill's College Custom Series consists of products that are produced from camera-ready copy. Peer review, class testing, and accuracy are primarily the responsibility of the author(s).

1 2 3 4 5 6 7 8 9 0 VNH VNH 0 9 8 7 6 5 4

ISBN 0-07-299342-1

Editor: Shirley Grall
Production Editor: Lynn Nagel
Cover Design: Cecil Williams
Printer/Binder: Von Hoffmann, Inc.

Acknowledgments

The Community Higher Education Council (CHEC) and the Local Education Agencies (LEA) Partnership for Reforming Teacher Education in South Carolina would like to express appreciation to the U.S. Department of Education for its support in the cost of producing this publication.

This publication was made possible and its content was reproduced with funds from a five year grant of $6.7 million awarded by the U.S. Department of Education's Teacher Quality Enhancement Program.

The editors wish to extend their gratitude to various individuals who contributed their valued technical assistance and suggestions to the preparation of this manuscript: Dr. Howard D. Hill, Dr. Calvin D. Hutson Jr., Dr. Carol Goodwin, Mrs. Sandra Garcia, Mrs. Rosemary Breeland, Mrs. Anne Tindall, Ms. Kim Ramsey, Mrs. Patricia Patterson, Dr. Sarah Washington-Favors, and Mrs. Joyce Williams.

A special note of appreciation and thanks to our educational partners who agreed to write specifically for this publication, and who worked diligently with us until its completion. Without their valued contributions this publication could not have been possible.

Dr. Earline M. Simms *Dr. Cash J. Kowalski* *Dr. Barbara J. O'Neal*

Table of Contents

Perspectives on Teacher Education Reform – Unique Partnership Initiatives

Dr. Earline M. Simms
Associate Vice President
for Academic Affairs
South Carolina State University

Introduction

Teacher education programs are being challenged and criticized by policy makers and much of the public for low quality of candidates admitted to teacher preparation programs, failure to connect programs to student and subject matter standards in k-12 schools, and for lacking academic rigor, among other issues.

In response to national education initiatives and new school mandates at the State level, k-12 schools, colleges and universities in Orangeburg, S.C. and other areas in the State, are partnering through a broad-based consortium to enhance student learning, preparing a higher caliber new-breed of teachers, and supporting our partnership teachers. The Community Higher Education Council (CHEC) brings together three institutions of higher learning: South Carolina State University (SCSU), a historically Black, public, senior comprehensive teaching, land-grant university; Claflin University (CU), a historically Black, private, broadly based liberal arts four-year institution; and Orangeburg-Calhoun Technical College (O-C Tech), and of South Carolina's 16 supported, two-year technical colleges. In addition, to these three institutions of higher learning, the partnership includes six local education agencies (LEAs): Calhoun County School District, Marion School District 7, Orangeburg Consolidated School Districts 3, 4 and 5, and Sumter School District 17.

The CHEC and LEAs partnership activities for reforming teacher education in South Carolina are supported by a five-year $6.7 million grant project funded by the U.S. Department of Education. Its purpose is to help teachers achieve proficiency in proven educational strategies and to pursue continuing education and National Board Certification. Hallmarks of the partnership are enhanced by teacher education programs with emphasis on performing effectively in a culturally and ethnically diverse society, technology to improve teaching, and become involved integrating in the community through service learning. The partnership's major goal is to develop a model for reforming teacher education by drawing on the unique strengths of each partner.

Through a collaborative relationship, the CHEC partnership conducts an array of activities designed to achieve its objectives: Enhance the teacher education programs at CU and SCSU by revising and aligning all teacher education curricula with INTASC and NCATE's professional standards and assessment processes of NBTS. Expand and enhance the pre-clincial and clinical experience of preservice teachers. Establish a network of Professional Development Schools (PDSs). Profile needs specific professional development for k-12 classroom teachers and university faculty. Expand the Beginning Teacher Assistance Program (BTAP). Develop the skills of preservice and in-service teachers and university faculty in using technology. Improve LEAs' student academic performance. Support National Board Certification for classroom teachers in partners LEAs. Establish centers for effective parenting. Improve the leadership skills of teachers, principals and superintendents.

The many benefits of the partnership to teachers, university faculty, students, parents, school districts, institutions of higher learning, and to our community and the state of South Carolina are substantial. Many of the initial accomplishments to date will continue to be nurtured, and will continue to flourish and bring enhanced benefits to all members of the Partnership in many years to come. Some of the highlights of the accomplishments and benefits to date can be validated by some of the achievements briefly listed below:

- Implemented reforms that hold teacher education programs accountable.
- Provided extensive training for prospective teachers to use technology as tool for teaching and learning.
- Strengthened the role of K-12 educators in the design of effective teacher education programs.
- Increased collaboration among administrators and faculty of higher edu cation institutions.
- Produced teachers with greater command of academic subjects and skills.
- Strengthened the pre-clinical experiences.

- Prepared teachers to work with diverse student populations.
- Increased parental involvement in partner LEA schools.
- Increased the diversity and number of teachers for partner LEA s.
- Increased the number of national board certified teachers in South Carolina.
- Enhanced the leadership skills of LEA principals.

Many of the accomplishments, initiatives underway and benefits of this teacher education quality enhancement project are described in this monograph: Perspectives On Teacher Education Reforms – Unique Partnership Initiatives in South Carolina. The monograph is comprised of numerous articles by collective members of the CHEC partnership, as well as by ten national leaders, who were invited to submit their perspectives on the importance of teacher education reform.

We are deeply indebted for the valuable contributions to this monograph by our partners, especially for the insightful and valuable perspectives by the state and national leaders who participated in this most important national project. The monograph promises to contribute to the contemporary literature on teacher education reform, a badly needed source of current information from national leaders and our partners.

An Interview with Dr. Richard Riley

U.S. Secretary of Education (1994-2001)

- *We face a diminishing pool of talent in our profession. What are some of the ways we could attract and retain quality personnel in teacher education?*

In South Carolina and in America, there is a dire crisis for quality teachers. There is also a great need for more quality teachers, teachers in fields like special education, bilingual education in math and science. The need is critical. As we look at attracting young people to teaching, it causes one to look at teacher education programs (schools/university systems where teachers are taught), in that schools of education do not collaborate well enough with the Schools of Arts and Sciences and, in many cases, higher education institutions don't recognize the School of Education as an equal partner. There is a great need for greater collaboration with the School of Education itself and within the university and those outside the university, to include collaborating with community colleges, which are very important, and collaborating with preschool right on through the 12th grade. What interests me about this model that is involved with South Carolina State University and the other partners is that it deals with these critical needs that are out there in the country and there in South Carolina. I think this project can provide tremendous help in resolving some of these major issues about providing a model that deals with these complications, which really are partnerships but which often are not dealt with.

- *There is a substantial increase of minority children in our public schools at a time when we face a decrease of minority teachers entering the profession. What could be done by the federal and/or state governments to attract more minority teachers?*

Teacher education personnel now have come to the front because of the crisis and the need for quality teachers, the need for partnerships and the great challenges out there. The Teacher Quality Enhancement grant, which comes from U. S. Department of Education, is a very solid grant, in my judgment. It gives South Carolina State University and Claflin University (a great

United Methodist Related University – I am a United Methodist and very proud of Claflin) a chance to work together and deal with this type of collaboration within the university system. I think that is so very important. I urge all people connected with both universities, not just the School of Education, to work to make sure that the School of Education is an equal partner with Arts and Sciences and that they work closely together and support each other. Your grant would call for that, in my judgement.

This collaboration with the community college, I think, is significant. The Orangeburg Calhoun Technical College gives you the opportunity to collaborate with a very important linkage of where many of the students come from who enter the field of education. An interesting statistic in America is that some 30% of the African-American teachers have come through the community college system. This is a very significant factor. If there is anything we need more of in America is more African-American teachers, males and females–in the preschool through K-12, and also in the colleges and universities. So the community college system is a wonderful way tc bring in future teachers. Collaboration with the community college, I think, can do so much.

A real critical part also in collaboration outside the university system is the wonderful opportunity to develop partnerships with the six school districts that are involved in this partnership. That is so critical because, from the school's standpoint, and also the education standpoint, this partnership is for developing teachers and also for serving school districts. Quality teachers are developed through valuable experiences in the classrooms, and being an integral part K-12 school partnership. If they are over here learning to be teachers and aren't involved in that process, they fall short of having a quality education to become a great teacher. So I am very pleased to see this partnership developed. I am familiar with those six school districts you are working with as partners, and I think that tremendous benefits can come from this partnership.

- *What are some of the accomplishments you feel were attributed to your tenure as US Secretary of Education?*

It is with interest to me that when I went to Washington (as Secretary of Education) and served President Clinton, education was not on the radar screen of most people. Education was supported, but not in a serious way. When President Clinton came out of office after eight years, education was the top issue in everybody's mind, in every poll in all geographic regions and all categories of people in America. I feel that President Clinton's leadership in education, and strongly supported by me, really made a difference in getting this country tuned into education, and was a very important factor for our future. The education standards movement, which I had supported in South Carolina in the mid-80's became adopted by all 50 states. Goals 2000 was the act that called for going out to the states to give them the money to build a standards process, including assessments, and it was passed in all 50 states. The standards movement is well and is working in every state, although we are having some reactions now because every state is different and testing is at a different level. The result is there is a reaction against so-called standardized tests and how it is taking too much of the creativity away from the teachers and taking too much time in the classroom to prepare the students for these tests. I think that is a serious concern and needs to be addressed. Although I don't think there is any simple answer to it, I do believe we need to revisit from time to time the issue of assessment, making sure it's fair and making sure students who are tested are prepared for the test. In short, the test must be on the material students have learned. I think they are not quite there yet and it is causing a great deal of controversy. So I hope we can work through that.

I am pleased, however, that the administration in Washington was able to get the country into the standards movement, that is defining what a child should know in 3rd grade science for example, making sure from preschool through the 3rd grade the child knows that and then moves forward. It is a simple process that works: we have to have assessments, it has to be fair, and we have to continually look at both standards and at assessments; and that is kind of where we are now. We need to step back and relook at all of that and make sure it is brought up to date and made fair.

- *What does the U.S. need to do to increase its standing in the world, as compared to other developed countries, i.e., Japan, Sweden, Germany, etc.?*

The best measure we have of comparison at the international level is so called TIMS Test and TIMS II. TIMS is the Third International Math/Science study. It is a good test, and it is a way for us to compare our students with students in other developed countries. What the TIMS test tells us is that in those early grades, through like the fourth or fifth grade, our students are doing very well. They do well on the basics; we score high, for example, in math and science in those early grades. At the end of the third grade, we are second only to South Korea in terms of science, and we are well above average in math. We begin getting into a problem is in the middle school years and then in the high school years. There are a number of reasons for that. One reason is that the TIMS study tells us is our curricula is a mile wide and inch deep. The Japanese in middle school, for example, would have maybe seven or eight topics they would develop in depth. In America, we might have thirty to thirty-five topics we develop thinly. It is a very interesting analysis to look at that, study it, and see why it is those students who seem to pull up in middle school and other students seem to lag behind, even though they were ahead in those elementary years. And then, of course, the same is true for high school. The studies show if young people are prepared in pre-algebra and algebra, then geometry and trigonometry, and if they then are prepared enough in pre-science courses to take the difficult courses in high school, this shows a real critical difference between the student who does well in college and life as far as education is concerned, and the one who does not. Those students who take calculus, trigonometry, biology, physics, and chemistry in high school usually become students who do very well. So we have a lot of work to do with preparing young people and giving them the background to get into these more difficult subjects as they move them through the school system. That would then certainly move us up in middle school, and high school where we are now falling short.

- *What are your thoughts about bringing people into education, even some on a part time basis, who are not educators by training (engineers, journalists, health professionals, etc.), but who would be interested in joining and making contributions at various levels of education?*

The recruitment of young people into teaching is a critical need in this country. It's a special critical need when it comes to attracting young minority students into the world of teaching. And that is so important for this country, and I have supported that all of my public life. I now feel stronger than ever on doing whatever it takes to attract young people and make them realize that the profession of teaching is a wonderful profession. However, certain characteristics of it have to be changed to make sure a young person sees that: 1) they will be compensated fairly for the professional work they will be doing and the kind of education it takes to get there; 2) their working conditions will be such that the teaching environment is a wonderful place to spend their day and, ultimately their life. We have to assure young people of these things and they have to see these things happening. For example, class size—we hear a lot of talk about class size. Class size is very important in terms of the teacher's working conditions in the classroom. If a teacher has 34-35 students, that is one kind of working condition. If a teacher has 18-20 students, that is entirely different. Now a teacher can work more individually with students, individual students, which is very important. All children learn differently, especially reading. It is so important for the teacher to be able to spend time with the individual child. Those kinds of things helps assure teachers they are not going to have a disruptive classroom. We need to provide young children, with the kind of teachers who will help them learn how to live with each other. There is a lot more to education than simply achieving high academic standards, as strong as I am for standards. Young people have to learn how to be good citizens; they have to learn about their government and about how they can play a role in their government. The U.S. is a democracy, where the people have the power, and the people need to be educated in order to properly use that power to make a great democracy work well. And that's part of education, especially public education. Therefore, I am very adamant about making all those things stronger and better. If we did this, we would have a natural effect of pulling more people, more African-Americans, men and women, into the teaching profession.

Message From the Governor State of South Carolina

Mark Sanford
Governor

Our children are our greatest asset and our hope for the future. That's why it is so important that we provide our teachers with the training and resources they need to provide quality educational opportunities for our students.

Teacher quality must be addressed through teacher education reform. This can be accomplished through changes in six major areas. First, all K-3 and special education teachers must receive training in explicit phonics in order to continue our reading initiatives. Explicit phonics teaches children the relationships between the letters of written language and the individual sounds of spoken language. By providing instruction in a set of letter-sound relationships and then organizing these relationships into a logical sequence, children learn to manipulate these relationships to use and write words. Moreover, knowing these relationships helps early readers recognize familiar words accurately and automatically and "decode" new words. Thus, explicit phonics contributes greatly to student ability to read words in isolation and in connected text.

Second, we need more mentorships. Teachers benefit from having a mentor and from mentoring others – not just while they are studying to become teachers, but throughout their careers. These types of reciprocal relationships promote broader academic experiences for our children and help ensure that teachers have the resources they need for guidance and support.

Third, colleges and universities need to allow more time for student internships in their teaching programs. For example, Furman University offers a 5-year program that truly provides hands-on experience for students studying to become teachers by combining internships with a strong mentoring program and academic instruction. The Furman Teacher to Teacher Program allows aspiring educators to develop their teaching abilities under the direct mentorship of some of our state's best and most experienced teachers. Elementary education candidates participate in a year-long internship, experiencing teaching in its real form while benefiting from practical advice and teaching tips. Another example is South Carolina State University's partnership with Claflin University, Orangeburg-Calhoun Technical College, and six area school districts to improve student services and reform teacher preparation. By encouraging these types of programs at colleges and universities throughout the state, we can improve teacher quality.

Fourth, we must remove the barriers teachers face in accessing continuing education. Distance learning provides a more economic method of high-quality instruction for teachers and students and is easily accessible through such outlets as SCETV, our technical colleges, and our four-year colleges and universities. This way, teachers get the training they need in their own venue – without having to travel.

Fifth, we must ensure that all our teachers have a bachelor's degree that demonstrates competence in their teaching area and that all teachers are certified in the area in which they are teaching. We must ensure that our teachers have the necessary basic skills and content knowledge to perform effectively. Our school children should have the best, most competent teachers available – teachers well-educated in the subject areas in which they are teaching. Subject area knowledge is important. However, subject area knowledge alone is not a sufficient measure of effective teaching. Teachers must also know how to teach. Combining basic skills and subject area certification will help promote the highest standards of teacher quality.

Finally, adopting a program that financially rewards teachers for the accomplishments of their students would increase teacher and student performance. Using student achievement as a measure of teacher competence creates a direct link between teacher quality and student success and ensures that those teachers who get the best results have an incentive to continuing teaching.

Though these six proposals for teacher education reform can make a difference in overall teacher quality, structural changes in teacher duties and responsibilities are also needed. Teachers need to have time to teach, and, unfortunately, their time is often consumed with heavy paperwork loads. Separating administrative functions and reducing teacher paperwork to only those documents related directly to student achievement would give teachers valuable time to plan and study so that they can provide our children with the best educational experience possible.

We also need to implement a plan to increase teacher salaries to the national average by 2009. Our teachers work hard and give their time and knowledge to prepare our young people for success. Raising teacher salaries is the only way to stabilize and strengthen teacher retention and keep quality people interested in teaching jobs in the Palmetto State. This is particularly true in rural areas where salaries remain low and teacher retention is a serious problem. Raising teacher salaries in rural areas would represent the first step in our goal of raising teacher salaries to the national average.

According to Education Week's "Quality Counts 2003," South Carolina's efforts to improve teacher quality are the best in the country. By continuing to work together to effect positive reforms in teacher education, we can ensure our enduring status as leaders in educational excellence.

Message from Congressman Clyburn

Congressman James E. Clyburn
(SC-6)

My first job following graduation from South Carolina State College was as a world history teacher at C.A. Brown High School in Charleston, South Carolina, in 1962. By all accounts, the students in my charge were not supposed to succeed. They are what we would now call "at-risk" students. However, these students had one thing working in their favor–dedicated teachers.

I sponsored a social club at C.A. Brown known as the Corsairs that helped give high achievers the tools to succeed in life. Obviously the group accomplished that goal because among the 10 club members are the United States Ambassador to Iceland, a Wall Street attorney, a Delaware State University executive, and the first black graduate of The Citadel. Working with the Corsairs is perhaps the thing of which I am most proud, because it was truly an experience in which I was able to personally affect lives for the better.

This is the unsung reward of the teaching profession – having the potential to impact the lives of so many individuals. There are numerous teachers today who experience the same sense of accomplishment from their careers. But like any job, you can only get back what you put into it. The quality of our teachers determines the quality of our schools. Our school systems shape all members of our society, and as a result our nation can only be as good as our school system.

South Carolina is on the right track. According to Education Week's annual Quality Counts Report South Carolina led the nation in its efforts to improve teacher quality. This achievement is the result of the priority former Governor Jim Hodges and State Education Superintendent Inez Tennenbaum placed on improving South Carolina's education system. Supporting higher teacher salaries, compensating National Board Certified teachers, and establishing an office of teacher recruitment have all contributed to the state's positive climate for improving teacher quality. Still there are other initiatives that have and can assist in further enhancing the pool of pre-service and in service education.

I have been pleased to play a role in the effort to recruit more qualified minorities to the teaching profession. In 2001, I secured $500,000 in federal funding for the Call Me Mister program, which is a collaborative effort between Clemson University and three of South Carolina's historically black colleges—Benedict College in Columbia, Claflin University in Orangeburg, and Morris College in Sumter. This is by all accounts, a stellar pro on these three campuses.

The program focuses on recruiting, training, certifying and securing employment for 200 African American males as elementary teachers in public schools. The ultimate goal of Call Me Mister is to develop a research-based model for national replication so that quantifiable results may be utilized in every state to improve the number of minority men entering the teaching profession This is even more crucial now as the need for positive male role models is growing exponentially.

There is another federally funded program, Troops to Teachers, in South Carolina that facilitates the transition of retired and separated members of the Armed Forces into teaching careers. Established in 1994, the program is a cooperative project between the U.S. Department of Education and the South Carolina Department of Education. In addition to placing former military personnel into classrooms, it provides support to educational districts that hire program participants.

The Troops to Teachers program has three main objectives: to help relieve teacher shortages, to provide positive role models for the nation's public school students, and to assist military personnel in their successful transition to teaching as a second career. This innovative effort allows former soldiers to utilize their real life experiences in a new way, effectively translating the discipline and determination of their military background into a positive academic experience for their students.

I believe Federal dollars are well spent on such innovative programs like Call Me Mister and Troops to Teachers. However, they only begin to address the need for improving teacher quality in South Carolina. The importance of community involvement in enhancing the state's educational system cannot be overstated. The inclusion of mentorship and recruitment programs sponsored by businesses, social and civic organizations and private citizens is paramount.

Sponsorship of such programs would enable school districts to recruit the best talent to the teaching vocation. Effective mentorship would also boost efforts to nurture the talent of the state's most promising teaching prospects, and I have the utmost confidence that we have the ability in this state to form substantial partnerships promoting the overall improvement of teacher quality.

Unfortunately, in tight budgetary years like we are experiencing now, teacher quality programs begin to suffer. The State Legislature is considering repealing the bonus paid to National Board Certified teachers in South Carolina, even though this incentive is a vital tool to keep the best teachers in the classroom now and into the immediate future. On the federal level, initiatives that help states and school districts reduce class sizes and better recruit and train teachers are in danger of significant funding cuts. We must maintain the commitment at all levels to insure our schools continue to have access to quality resources and intellectual capital.

I am keenly aware of the challenges facing educators today. My daughter, Jennifer, is an educator currently serving as a Reading Specialist for Richland School District Two. Her experiences in the classroom, mirror many of those I had nearly 30 years ago. These shared experiences are the basis for my commitment to improving teacher quality.

The effectiveness of a teacher has been shown through research to have a direct relationship to student achievement, and many of our lowest paid administrators still make more than some of our highest paid teachers. It's rime to exalt our teachers for the great impact they have on our children and to congratulate those who choose this honored field as their profession. Tight budgets are no excuse to undermine the future of our children, our state and our nation.

Keeping Our Eyes on the Prize: Teacher Education Reform in South Carolina

Inez M. Tenenbaum,
State Superintendent of Education
South Carolina

South Carolina is now seeing the tangible results of an intense four-year effort to bring about reforms in teacher education in this state. I fully concur with Frederick Douglass's observation, "If there is no struggle, there is no progress." We have struggled courageously, even heroically, toward teacher education reform, and I am very pleased to report that we are indeed making progress. Our SAT scores have improved at the highest rate in the nation. Education Week's Quality Counts 2003 ranks South Carolina best in the country for improving teacher quality. We rank twelfth in the nation for raising academic standards. In 1999, South Carolina had nineteen teachers who were certified by the National Board for Professional Teaching Standards. Today, we have 2,358 National Board-certified teachers—a total that puts our state third in the nation. This is an exciting time for South Carolina's teachers and students. But the journey continues. As Robert Frost wrote, "I have promises to keep, and miles to go before I sleep."

My journey toward substantial, meaningful teacher education reform began in 1999, when I was sworn in as South Carolina's Superintendent of Education. The state's former governor, and my dear friend, Richard Riley was then serving as the able and innovative Secretary of Education in the Clinton administration. Jim Hodges, who had run on a strong education platform, was being inaugurated as the state's governor. Members of both South Carolina's House and Senate had expressed deep concern and had voiced a commitment to improving the quality of education in the state's public schools. The time was ripe for innovative teacher education reform.

I knew then that South Carolina could not hesitate to follow the lead of the National Commission on Teaching and America's Future, which had asserted in 1996 in a landmark report, "A caring, competent, and qualified teacher for every child is the most important ingredient in education reform." I also knew that such a goal, though a tough one, was attainable. As we reviewed the state's teacher education standards, we discovered that they were, in some cases, twenty to twenty-five years old. Clearly, teachers who had graduated from the institutions that were using these outdated standards were finding themselves in many ways unprepared for the challenges they faced in the classroom. And this lack of adequate teacher preparation was impeding the academic progress of South Carolina's public school students. Soon, our desire to place a competent, caring, and qualified teacher in every classroom became more than a vision. It became our rallying cry.

In July 2000, I created a new division at the State Department of Education that would be devoted to improving teacher quality within our state. Dr. Janice Poda, former director of the South Carolina Center for Teacher Recruitment, was hired to lead the Division of Teacher Quality. Dr. Poda's team was charged with rewriting and updating the state's teacher education program standards and aligning them with national standards. In addition, Dr. Poda was to oversee teacher certification, Title II Higher Education Grants, the state's program for Assisting, Developing, and Evaluating Professional Teaching (ADEPT), and the Program of Alternative Certification for Educators (PACE).

In the mid-1990s, the State Department of Education and the Commission on Higher Education entered into a partnership with the National Council for Accreditation of Teacher Education (NCATE), the result of which was the requirement that all teacher education programs in South Carolina's public colleges and universities earn NCATE accreditation. But because the private institutions of higher education in the state can choose not to seek to be accredited by NCATE, a dual system of accreditation for the state's teacher education programs was created. We quickly realized, therefore, that South Carolina needed to move away from its dated input-based system of accrediting teacher education programs for all institutions to one that took a serious look at performance-based education. We again turned to NCATE–a leader in accreditation issues designed to improve the preparation of the nation's teachers, educational leaders, and other professional specialists–as our model. We found that NCATE had spent the past decade strengthening its standards and procedures by establishing a new system oriented to teacher candidate performance.

NCATE had created six standards for the accreditation of colleges and universities that prepare teachers and other professional personnel for work in elementary and secondary schools. These standards, which look at the overall program to prepare teachers, are as follows:

I. CANDIDATE PERFORMANCE

Standard 1: *Candidate Knowledge, Skills, and Dispositions*

Candidates preparing to work in schools as teachers or other professional school personnel know and demonstrate the content, pedagogical, and professional knowledge, skills, and dispositions necessary to help all students learn. Assessments indicate that candidates meet professional, state, and institutional standards.

Standard 2: *Assessment System and Unit Evaluation*

The unit has an assessment system that collects and analyzes data on the applicant qualifications, candidate and graduate performance, and unit operations to evaluate and improve the unit and its programs.

II. UNIT CAPACITY

Standard 3: *Field Experiences and Clinical Practice*

The unit and its school partners design, implement, and evaluate field experiences and clinical practice so that teacher candidates and other school personnel develop and demonstrate the knowledge, skills, and dispositions necessary to help all students learn.

Standard 4: *Diversity*

The unit designs, implements, and evaluates curriculum and experiences for candidates to acquire and apply the knowledge, skills, and dispositions necessary to help all students learn. These experiences include working with diverse higher education and school faculty, diverse candidates, and diverse students in P–12 schools.

Standard 5: *Faculty Qualifications, Performance, and Development*

Faculty are qualified and model best professional practices in scholarship, service, and teaching, including the assessment of their own effectiveness as related to candidate performance. They also collaborate with colleagues in the disciplines and schools. The unit systematically evaluates faculty performance and facilitates professional development.

Standard 6: *Unit Governance and Resources*

The unit has the leadership, authority, budget, personnel, facilities, and resources, including information technology resources, for the preparation of candidates to meet professional, state, and institutional standards.

(The full text of NCATE's performance-based accreditation standards can be found on-line at <http://www.ncate.org.>)

With input from teacher educators, teachers, parents, business people, and other educators from across the state, we also set about to review, rewrite, and update the content area standards for all teacher education programs in the state of South Carolina. For many of the content areas, the subcommittees of the Teacher Education Performance-Based Standards Committee elected to adopt the national standards as the South Carolina standards. All of these national standards were developed by the professional associations and scholarly societies for the various disciplines. The subcommittees for several other program areas chose to develop original standards for South Carolina teacher education. Still other area subcommittees chose to use a combination of national and state standards, either by writing a set of standards that meld the two or by adopting the national standards in addition to formulating a new set of original standards.

In addition, we sought to align our program standards in teacher education with our preK–12 state curriculum standards. For example, because the standards established by the National Council of Teachers of Mathematics (NCTM) were found by the mathematics subcommittee to be very closely aligned with the South Carolina curriculum standards, we adopted the NCTM standards as the state's standards for mathematics. The national standards that have now been adopted for fourteen of South Carolina's areas of certification are NCATE approved. The State Board of Education adopted the new South Carolina teacher education program standards in the summer of 2002.

Currently, all public teacher education programs in South Carolina must be reviewed by teams from NCATE and its specialty professional associations as well as by state evaluation teams. All teacher education programs, in both public and private institutions, are evaluated every five years on the basis of NCATE and state standards (non-NCATE accredited institutions are evaluated by state teams only). To date, teacher education programs in thirty institutions in South Carolina have received approval. Two institutions are currently developing teacher education programs. Eleven public institutions and seven private institutions in our state are now accredited by NCATE.

As part of the teacher education reforms, we are in the process of transitioning to four certificate grade spans for our teachers: early childhood, elementary, middle, and secondary. These levels ensure that teacher education programs provide specific training designed to meet the unique needs of children within each grade level.

Our Title II higher education report card requires teacher education programs to be accountable for their candidates' performance on the national tests Praxis I (basic skills), Praxis II content area exams, and Principles of Learning and Teaching. In addition, teacher education programs must submit assessment plans explaining how they will ensure that all candidates meet the standards. Going beyond the data required by the United States Department of Education for the higher education report card, South Carolina has developed a new state accountability system that looks at candidates' test scores as well as their performance in the classroom. We also intend to carefully examine the results of employer surveys to help us determine whether first- and second-year teachers are, in fact, well prepared to perform in the classroom.

As we continue to make significant improvements, we find that the old adage "the only constant is change" indeed holds true. The Bush administration and Congress have instituted a wide-reaching reform in teacher education with the No Child Left Behind (NCLB) Act, which requires a "highly" qualified teacher in each classroom in America by the end of 2005–06. Fortunately, building on the strength of Richard Riley's initiatives and our four years of reform, we find ourselves poised to move ahead with the NCLB and are currently working closely with the state's colleges and universities as well as district superintendents, personnel directors, and our forty-five-thousand-strong teacher workforce. We have every intention of providing a caring, competent, and highly qualified teacher to each and every South Carolina student by 2006.

While teacher education reform and teacher quality have demanded our urgent attention, we have not neglected other areas of education reform. During the past four years our schools have experienced a significant decrease in violent crime. I had the pleasure of working with Governor Hodges in the creation of South Carolina's successful First Steps initiative, which gave preschoolers throughout the state an opportunity to start school ready to learn. As a result, more South Carolina children are testing ready for school than ever before. In addition, we have led a successful effort to provide over $750 million for school construction without raising taxes. We have reduced class size, created more alternative schools, raised teachers' salaries, and provided more guidance counselors and resource officers for our schools. I am also proud of the creation of the School Leadership Executive Institute, which trains our principals and superintendents.

In January of 2003, I was sworn in for a second term as South Carolina's Superintendent of Education. Governor Sanford accepted my invitation to meet and discuss the future of education in our state. During the next four years I look forward to partnering with the Governor, the General Assembly, State Board members, college and university deans, district superintendents, State Department of Education staff members, and, of course, the thriving professionals who are South Carolina's teachers. We must, as the Civil Rights anthem admonishes us, keep our "eyes on the prize"– which, in our case, is the highest possible level of achievement by the students in South Carolina's public schools.

Superintendent

Inez Tenenbaum

A Message from the Past Governor of South Carolina

Jim Hodges

In 1983 the National Commission on Excellence in Education published a report entitled *A Nation at Risk: The Imperative for Education Reform* which jolted states into action. One focus of this report was the need for rigorous evaluation and improvement of teacher education in the colleges and universities of the nation. The first two paragraphs of A Nation at Risk issued to every state a jarring and unforgettable warning that "The educational foundations of our society are presently being eroded by a rising tide of mediocrity that threatens our very future as a nation and a people."

If we are going to combat mediocrity in our education system and prepare South Carolina to compete in a global marketplace, we must advance teacher education reform.

I believe that one of the most significant impacts in promoting accountability in teacher education has come from the National Council for the Accreditation of Teacher Education (NCATE), the premier national accrediting body in teacher education. NCATE, which is inclusive of a body of organizations such as the American Association of Colleges and for Teacher Education (AACTE), Council of Chief State School Officers, and National School Boards Association, to name a just a few, developed a shared vision of teacher education. NCATE has evolved a set of continuously updated, quality standards in areas of evaluation that are critical to the preparation of teachers.

In June of 1999, I appointed an eighteen member Governor's Commission on Teacher Quality and charged them with developing policy recommendations regarding the improvement of teacher training, recruitment, retention, certification and professional development. The Commission recognized that this ambitious agenda could only be accomplished through a partnership of all stakeholders. Both public and higher education constituencies contributed to a renewed focus on teacher quality. The emphasis on improving instruction was evidenced by South Carolina's designation as the national leader in improving teacher quality in the "Quality Counts 2003" issue of *Education Week.*

Many of the recommendations included in the Commission's initial report were also included in *Senate Bill !!!*, which I signed into law. This omnibus teacher quality bill will require an additional three days annually of professional development for teachers and special certification for teachers going into the middle grades. I also supported new laws that create teacher incentives for more qualified individuals to go into teaching. These laws will provide teachers with 28 years retirement, higher salaries, and increase of $7,500 for those who become nationally certified through the National Board of Professional Teacher Standards.

If our State is going to continue to progress in education we cannot diminish our efforts to improve our teacher education programs. Teachers who are knowledgeable, competent, and well prepared to each will provide our classrooms with the level of professionalism our children need and deserve.

Sincerely,

Jim Hodges

Jim Hodges

Performance-Based Accreditation: Reform in Action

Dr. Arthur E. Wise
President, NCATE
National Council for Accreditation of Teacher Education

Policymakers are searching for ways to scale up school and higher education reforms that are happening in small pockets across America. Creating lasting change is a huge challenge. Because of its requirements relating to P-12 student testing, which have ramifications for schools, districts, states, and higher education institutions alike, the No Child Left Behind Act will leave its mark on American education for years to come.

Similarly, the National Council for Accreditation (NCATE) system is institutionalizing reforms in teacher preparation which are helping to create new norms of behavior around reform ideas and concepts.

NCATE is not merely an accrediting agency–it is a force for the reform of teacher preparation. As institutions meet the performance-based standards of NCATE, they are reforming themselves. NCATE's expectations for teacher preparation institutions are a radical change from input and process-oriented standards of the past.

For example, in NCATE's performance-based system, accreditation is based on results–results that demonstrate that the teacher candidate knows the subject matter and can teach it effectively so that students learn. In the NCATE system, it is no longer good enough for a faculty member or a teacher candidate to say, "I taught the material." The focus is on showing that the candidate can actually connect theory to practice and be effective in an actual P-12 classroom. Subject matter knowledge may be assessed by PRAXIS or another content knowledge test, and this information is used in the accreditation decision. But other measures of candidate content knowledge are used as well. NCATE examiners assess how well the candidate can synthesize the content to help P-12 students understand it.

In addition, the college must have a system in place to assess its candidates. This system must include assessments at entry, throughout the program, and upon exit. Benchmarks for acceptable learning must also be set, and institutions must have evidence that candidates who are recommended for licensure have performed at acceptable levels. NCATE has established rubrics for institutions to use to help them determine satisfactory levels of performance, and will be developing additional rubrics in content areas.

NCATE standards also expect teacher educators to model effective teaching. The traditional lecture alone is inadequate. Teacher educators must use strategies that they expect their candidates to use. Why? Teachers teach as they are taught. Teacher educators should model expert teaching.

In addition, accredited colleges of education also expect candidates to demonstrate that they can teach students of diverse backgrounds. Many sessions on working with diverse populations have been held at annual conferences; institutions routinely swap information on approaches to recruiting a diverse student population and a diverse faculty; and the new standards continue the expectation that candidates should be prepared to help all students learn.

At accredited institutions candidates should be able to use technology effectively as a teaching tool. Just seven years ago, technology was on the periphery of teacher preparation, but in NCATE's 1995 standards, technology began to play an important role. In the past seven years, deans have been preparing technology plans for their units; regional workshops on technology integration have been held; and institutions know that technology is an essential teaching tool–it's here to stay. Now, NCATE standards expect the use of technology to be central to teacher preparation in the 21st century and beyond.

The clinical program in teacher preparation is changing rapidly, and NCATE has served to help institute change in this area. The performance-based NCATE system requires university and P-12 school faculty to function as partners in the education of teacher candidates. The higher education and P-12 faculty must collaboratively design and implement the program for teacher candidates. The emphasis on interacting as partners is far-reaching and profound. Cooperating P-12 teachers and supervisors have traditionally been treated as peripheral in the higher education arena. Now they are expected to be central figures in the planning and implementation process. A change in culture is taking place in higher education and in P-12 schools. The movement was started by the Holmes Group as it fostered the idea of professional development schools. NCATE has integrated many of the concepts inherent in the PDS into expectations for the clinical programs at accredited institutions, and is "mainstreaming" the reform.

A powerful sign that these concepts are now embedded into the expectations of the field is that the language of the NCATE standards has been adapted and adopted as state standards in most states. NCATE has partnerships with 46 states and two jurisdictions to strengthen teacher preparation and reduce duplication of effort when institutions undergo state program and review for professional accreditation purposes.

Where does South Carolina stand? NCATE and South Carolina have a three-way partnership that includes the State Department of Education and the Commission of Higher Education. Of a total of 31 teacher preparation institutions in South Carolina, 22 are in the NCATE system, either accredited (19) or as candidates (3), for a total of 71 percent of the state's institutions affiliated with NCATE. That number has evolved during the past six years under the direction of South Carolina's education leaders. South Carolina has adopted/adapted NCATE standards as its state standards. Furthermore, at accredited institutions in South Carolina, NCATE conducts the review of the college of education using its performance-based unit standards. In addition, the specialty program areas (i.e. math, science, social studies preparation) are reviewed by specialists in that field who use national association program standards (for example, National Council of Teachers of Mathematics standards) that NCATE has recognized in its system. The state uses evidence from NCATE's findings in making independent state approval decisions for the college of education and its specific programs. South Carolina uses NCATE as a resource and works together with NCATE as a partner in strengthening its teacher preparation programs.

As institutions become accredited, they become part of a system of quality assurance in the teaching profession. Accreditation standards are now aligned with model state licensing standards and advanced certification standards. Too, licensing assessments are now being aligned with the profession's standards. One would think that this alignment would have occurred long ago. Licensing tests were not common until a decade ago, and they were initially developed by private companies with minimal input from the field. The teaching profession's standards should be the core of licensing examinations.

In addition, institutions are also redesigning advanced master's degrees to incorporate the standards of the National Board for Professional Teaching Standards. This move is strengthening existing master's degrees as they revise their programs. New and revised programs will focus on improving teaching skills in specific subject areas. This dramatic and coming change in master's degree programs aligned with NBPTS standards means increased professionalism and competence among experienced teachers. As more teachers become acquainted with the standards of the NBPTS, more will seek Board certification.

This alignment among accreditation, licensing, and advanced certification standards will play out in higher education institutions as the institutions ensure that their graduates will perform at an acceptable level. The alignment will eventually provide evidence of the common body of knowledge that all teachers should know as the assessments are revised to reflect the profession's standards. It certainly will bring more coherence to quality assurance efforts in the teaching profession.

NCATE's expectations weave many of the reforms of the 1980s and 1990s into one piece of cloth—the concepts embedded in professional development schools; the measures of effective teaching in specific subject areas through the National Board standards; the alignment of licensing examinations with teacher preparation standards; making teacher preparation a "real world" experience. Many institutions are not where they should be yet, but the direction in which they are headed is clear. Performance-based accreditation requires organizational change and development on the part of all involved.

Policymakers can encourage unaccredited teacher preparation institutions to move toward meeting NCATE standards as a way to ensure better teacher quality, and develop support and incentives for institutions to achieve professional NCATE accreditation. As more institutions meet NCATE's national professional standards, more qualified teacher candidates will be available, since candidates from accredited institutions pass licensing examinations at a significantly higher rate than do those from unaccredited institutions or those with no teacher preparation. Encouraging schools of education to attain national professional accreditation will increase the supply of well-qualified teacher candidates who can improve student achievement.

A Look at the State of Teacher Education in the United States[1]

Dr. David G. Imig
President/CEO, AACTE
American Association of Colleges of Teacher Education

Traditional teacher education programs are being challenged everywhere[2]. Criticisms range from the low quality of candidates admitted to preparation programs to the lack of subject-matter preparation. Teacher preparation is criticized for its failure to connect preparation programs to student and subject matter standards in K-12 schools, for lacking academic rigor and being disconnected from real-life school experiences. Teacher educators are being challenged to show the value-added of teacher education and the efficacy of different models (four vs. five vs. fifth year programs) and approaches (child centered vs. teacher centered). Teacher education is criticized for the fragmented nature of programs. These criticisms are compounded by the perception that traditional programs have failed to produce sufficient numbers of beginning teachers to overcome a persistent demand for more and more high quality teachers for hard to staff schools in rural and urban areas of the country.

Policy makers, who today are riveted on the promise of high quality teaching, are often dismissive of traditional teacher education programs they believe are ineffectual. The fact that teacher education is often over-regulated and under-resourced is ignored. In many jurisdictions, policy makers set admission criteria into programs and prescribe outcomes for graduates. They often dictate the content to be learned, prescribe the number of courses to be taken, and determine the examinations to be used before candidates can be licensed. They contend that candidate performance must be measured in multiple ways but rely on single measures - scores of candidates on standardized tests - to render policy decisions.

While much of the policy debate about teacher education in the United States originated at the state level, it has shifted to the federal level as a result

1 This paper is an excerpt taken from a speech delivered at the Japanese Association of Colleges for Teacher Education's Annual Meeting in Naruto, Tokoshima, Japan on October 12, 2002

2 Traditional teacher education is a phrase assigned to collegiate-based preparation programs by policy makers. It is a phrase emphatically rejected by the AACTE community who describe their work in the context of professional preparation.

of the nationalization of teacher education policy over the past two decades. Today it finds its voice in policy proposals articulated by the Bush administration. While these proposals represent a bold reach by the federal government into a traditional state prerogative, namely the setting of policy for the approval of teacher education programs and the licensure of teachers, these policy proposals are being endorsed by policy makers at the state level. Using funding authorized in Title II, Part A of the No Child Left Behind Act of 2001 (P.L. 107-110), federal lawmakers intend to see these federal proposals translated into state actions that will dramatically reshape teacher education. Nearly $3 billion has been awarded to states and local school districts to address issues of high quality teaching. These efforts are certain to be reinforced by successive efforts that will be included in the forthcoming reauthorization of Individuals with Disabilities Education Act (IDEA) and the next reauthorization of the Higher Education Act. If fully enacted, these policy proposals would redirect existing federal support from traditional teacher education to alternative providers, including local school districts, seriously impairing the capacity of education schools to prepare and support sufficient numbers of high quality beginning teachers.

Those policy proposals were made in a report to the Congress by the U.S. Department of Education on the quality of teacher education programs, as mandated by Title II of the Higher Education Act of 1998 (P.L. 105-750). Entitled The Secretary's Annual Report on Teacher Quality. Meeting the Highly Qualified Teachers Challenge, the June 2002 report offers four broad policy proposals that would affect education schools and/or traditional preparation program (Paige 2002):

- support the development of new models of "teacher training" that are "local," "based on the best alternative route programs of today," and "pro duce teachers with those skills that are in high demand" by local schools
- support state initiatives to end the "exclusive franchise" of schools of education and to curtail the "shocking number of ...mandated... education courses to qualify for certification" or assist state efforts to uncouple education school courses from state licensure and make "attendance at schools of education...optional"
- help states to "streamline" licensure requirements to place a premium on verbal ability and content knowledge, develop new and "challenging assessments" for teacher candidates, and require "content area majors for prospective teachers"
- promote state efforts to shift authority for determining the qualifications of beginning teachers "from state certification officials...to local school principals"

- These policy proposals are based on a set of claims that have been widely embraced by conservative scholars, policy makers and news media. These claims include:
- "rigorous research indicates that verbal ability and content knowledge are the most important attributes of highly qualified teachers"
- "there is little evidence that education school course work leads to improved student achievement"
- "today's certification system discourages some of the most talented candidates from entering the profession while allowing too many poorly qualified individuals to teach"
- "alternative routes to certification demonstrate that streamlined systems can boost the quantity of teachers while maintaining - or even improving - their quality."

For an administration that has repeatedly pressed for research evidence to be "scientifically based," little of such evidence is used to substantiate this set of claims. The reports and studies that are cited have a decidedly ideological bent, were primarily funded by a single source, and fail the requirement for being peer reviewed or relying on randomized experiments. The Paige report, which was ostensibly about the performance of education schools in meeting Title II, Sec. 207 requirements of the Higher Education Act as amended in 1998, gives little attention to the matter of candidate performance or the pass rates of candidates enrolled in education schools. It essentially dismisses the Congressional mandate to do so and asserts that while "the vast majority of teacher preparation program completers are passing the assessments required by their states for certification, "the reason for this is that the "rigor" of the state teacher tests "fall far short." The report asserts that low cut scores and "10th-grade level" tests characterize the current system of teacher licensure with the "academic standards for teachers, in far too many states" being "extremely low." In a well-orchestrated companion piece, issued by The Education Trust, an additional claim is made that the favorable picture the data portray is due to the fact that institutions and states are issuing reports that, "if not technically dishonest, are surely misleading" (Huang and Haycock (2002).

Still another claim that is buried in the Secretary's report is that "schools of education and formal training programs are failing to produce the types of high quality teachers that *No Child Left Behind Act* demands." This is a serious assertion because it suggests that a major impediment to the implementation of this massive proposal for restructuring American education is the lack of teachers sufficiently grounded in standards, assessments and the teaching of all students. While the legislation and the subsequent rule making by the Education Department offer a definition of a highly qualified teacher with much detail, the Assistant Secretary for the Office of Educational Research and Improvement, Grover Whitehurst, has offered a definition that appears to constitute the policy direction to be pursued by the Bush administration. Whitehurst has stated that the success of *No Child Left Behind Act* is dependent upon "good enough teachers" who are skilled at teaching a lesson, maintaining discipline, and ensuring that students do well on whatever performance measure is used. His is an advocacy for the technician teacher, different from the professional teacher, prepared at the school site and focused on implementing the specific curriculum of that school. In other words, he advocates skill based training and a view of teaching as a skilled occupation rather than a learned profession. He suggests that the professional teacher, prepared in traditional teacher education programs is a luxury we cannot afford. Whitehurst contends that professional teachers use little of what is provided in a professional preparation program and present a costly burden to high needs schools[3].

Progress of the Past Ten Years – An Era of Accomplishment

In some sense it is ironic that this divergence between policy makers and so-called traditional providers should occur at this time. While criticism of teacher education has existed for decades education schools used the 1990s to make fundamental changes, much of it guided by new scholarship and informed practice. Traditional programs have:

- Transformed the undergirding belief system of teacher education from behaviorism to constructivism and associationism and from a teacher centered to student centered emphasis
- Moved more and more of the professional preparation program into well designed and extensive clinical experiences in K-12 schools and away from the university – experimenting with Professional Development Schools designed to fully integrate academic and clinical preparation for beginning teachers – and other forms of partnerships
- Met the need for a new category of teacher- to staff middle schools (grades 5-8) – who possess greater mastery of content knowledge
- Transformed preparation to focus on standards based schooling with greater emphasis on student learning and subject matter knowledge – aligning teacher education to local, state and national content standards

3 Whitehurst made his statement at both the AACTE/CBE/STEP Conference, held in Washington, DC, June 6-9, 2002 and at a Research Seminar, held at the Carnegie Foundation for the Advancement of Teaching in Palo Alto, CA, June 10-12, 2002.

for students - and redid methods courses to emphasize pedagogical con tent knowledge.

- Experimented with case methods and new forms of clinical practice, problem-based service learning and on comprehensive or integrated services - as part of the curriculum.
- Reengaged academics who teach the academic disciplines in a dialogue about their responsibilities for teacher education and the need for stronger content knowledge for prospective teachers (and promoted conversations about the all-university responsibility for teacher education)
- Put more and more emphases on new forms of accountability - measuring the performance of teacher candidates using tests of content knowledge - and recast our accreditation system to drive the movement
- Incorporated technology training as a part of the teacher education curriculum -making major purchases of both hardware and software - and mounted numerous experiments using new forms of technology to connect teacher candidates to teacher educators at various stages of their preparation and practice.
- Experienced the politicization of the pedagogy surrounding mathematics, reading and bilingual education and responded with new approaches to the teaching of these subjects.
- Focused greater attention on the learning needs of low income and ethnically diverse students by greatly increasing the clinical experiences of teacher candidates in high needs schools and recasting foundations courses to focus on multiculturalism.
- Aligned post-baccalaureate training to the design principles, expectations and advanced standards of the National Board for Professional Teaching Standards (NBPTS)
- Raised admission requirements repeatedly - seeking more highly qualified students - and gained a cohort of more able teacher candidates, particularly at the secondary level.
- Invested enormous sums in the strengthening of special education programs and the preparation of all teachers to meet the expectations of special needs children and youth
- Experimented with program diversification or alternative preparation models - adopting new program designs intended to cater to the needs of particular candidates (often those with prior degrees and working

experiences) and emphasized preparation to teach particular student populations (urban, rural, Limited English Proficiency, etc.)

- Diversified the faculty and transformed the teacher candidate pool to give greater attention to the racial, linguistic and ethnic diversity of K-12 schools.

It is our contention that these changes had a positive and profound impact on the quality of beginning teachers who graduated from colleges and universities.

Five Shortcomings

We also did some things in the 1990s that have had adverse consequences. During the decade we increasingly focused on outcomes or performance expectations – and away from qualitative considerations (now called input measures) – with the result that we created a basis for competition with the array of alternative providers that emerged outside the universities. In the process, we failed to heed the warnings of many that we needed to emphasize the quality of the faculty and the integrity of the program, the philosophical underpinnings of the program and its purposes, the interactions promoted by cohort groupings and clinical formats – the conditions typically afforded by university cultures and, instead, succumbed to the pressure to focus on performance outcomes. While traditional providers were the ones who established the definitions of performance and practice they also created the condition for the current competition between alternative and traditional providers. They allowed alternative preparation programs to compete based on outcome and not input with the result that some alternatives were able to prepare beginning teacher in shorter periods of time and lower costs using the measures we created to claim high quality

A second thing that happened in the past decade is that we situated the bulk of teacher education in the schools and relied on practitioners, K-12 teachers, to do much of the training. More than half of the professional preparation of a teacher – as measured by clock hours – now takes place in K-12 schools. While the teachers we prepared in this way were highly skilled and ready to practice, the unintended consequence was that we validated the claim that the best form of preparation is to put teacher candidates in schools and let them learn from mentor teachers.

A third thing we did was to push social foundations out of the curriculum and allow the perception that our traditional social progressivism had been radicalized to go unchallenged. The center-left liberalism of teacher educators-with their advocacy for democratic institutions and the full inclusion of all students - rankled many right-of-center conservatives. Conservatives questioned the so-called social justice agenda of most education schools and Diane Ravitch's (2000) Left Back asserted that attention to these concerns resulted in too little attention to student learning by education schools and the result was the failure of the public schools. These claims were repeated in conservative circles and tempted political conservatives, who dominated policy making for teacher education in many states to further regulate the content and substance of teacher education programs. Conservative policy makers demanded an end to the "massive number of education courses" and the "political indoctrination" of teacher candidates in teacher education programs. This challenge has not been resolved, and there are often intense disagreements within education schools about the necessary prominence of the so-called social justice agenda versus the focus on K-12 student learning.

Fourth, in the name of professionalism we sought to emulate the preparation of physicians and lawyers - to create well educated professionals willing and able to diagnose learning needs and prescribe and administer remedies – through robust university-based programs that were to be five and six years in length. We attempted to do this at a time when the focus shifted from seat-time to performance expectations – when policymakers were seeking cost economies and scaling back university preparation programs. The result was often under-subscribed courses and challenges to the maintenance of extended programs - despite evidence that graduates of such programs were better prepared and stayed longer in teaching.

Fifth, we allowed the rhetoric of teacher shortage to shape the policy discourse - despite the fact that we produced almost two million new teachers in the 1990s we allowed politicians to believe that a terrible and long-term shortage of teachers would occur and let this dominate the policy discourse. The intention was that the policy makers, fearing teacher shortages, would respond with adjustments in the salaries and conditions of beginning teachers and with increased investments in traditional preparation programs. Instead, the policy community responded by sponsoring non-collegiate based alternative preparation programs that were low cost and of short duration.

These conditions have led us to a situation that is unprecedented. Describing traditional preparation programs in university based education schools as "failing" and assigning them the blame for low quality teachers, the Bush administration has now signaled their intention to make major changes in the form and substance of teacher preparation. Their advocacy is for a new model of teacher preparation to prepare technician teachers, or as Assistant Secretary Grover Russ Whitehurst suggested, "good enough" teachers. As noted above, the Bush administration has launched a series of policy directives that would force changes in state teacher education policies – the place where policy has traditionally been set for teacher education. These include:

States being encouraged to change their rules for licensure requiring no more than a university degree in the subject to be taught and some assurance that beginning teacher are "safe to practice"

States being encouraged to promote alternative preparation routes that are school based, of short duration and focused on the curriculum of a particular school or school district.

States being encouraged to "investigate" university based preparation programs to ensure that their curriculum corresponds to scientifically based research evidence (and to close those that do not)

States being encouraged – often with incentives – to refocus candidate performance expectations away from program completion and toward successful practice – using new value added assessment techniques to identify effective teachers.

The Bush administration has also forced changes on the specialized accreditation agency agenda that sets professional standards for teacher education programs – National Council for Accreditation of Teacher Education – relegating all standards to a place of less importance than candidate performance on a test of subject matter knowledge – the so-called Title II test. (The Education Department has also supported the development of new teacher tests that would focus much greater attention on subject matter knowledge and classroom management). The Bush administration has also eliminated several federal grant programs that have provided substantial monies to traditional programs and shifted these funds to professional development programs that are situated in local schools and school districts. The Bush administration has also defined teacher professional development in ways that will challenge, if not eliminate most traditional programs from competing with for-profit providers of such services.

So What Is Likely to Occur?

In this kind of policy environment, what is likely to occur?

- Education schools will be challenged to more closely align their programs and offerings to the needs of local schools and school districts resulting in a narrowing of mission and purpose (and programs).
- Faculties inside education schools, absent state frameworks for preparation programs, will have to agree on the components of their programs and what is necessary to make it marketable. Outside or external

endorsements of quality will become useful markers in the marketing of programs.

- Education schools will identify research agendas and scholarly activities and invest in those that are intended to benefit the image of the program and its marketability
- Economies of scale and per candidate costs will become primary concerns as education schools must generate resources to pay for their infrastructure
- Entrepreneurial characteristics of faculty will come to be valued as much as traditional values of teaching, research and service
- In this kind of policy environment some education schools will thrive while others will be diminished or even eliminated

We are in for very interesting and challenging times because this policy agenda is likely to prevail and with it fundamental change in the way we prepare teachers for K-12 schools - particularly in an era of standards and high stakes testing. Gearing university based preparation programs to connect in meaningful ways with the needs of local schools and school districts is our future - the needs of local schools (and their communities) are our mission. Transforming education schools to focus on local teachers, principals, parents and students is the challenge.

References

Huang, S., Yi, Y., & Haycock, K. (2002). Interpret With Caution: The First State Title II Reports on the Quality of Teacher Preparation. Washington, DC: The Education Trust.

Paige, Roderick. (2002) *Meeting the Highly Qualified Teachers Challenge: The Secretary's Annual Report on Teacher Quality.* U.S. Department of Education, Office of Postsecondary Education. Washington, DC

Ravitch, Diane. (2000). *Left Back.* Simon & Schuster. New York.

Creating the Context for School/University Reform of Teacher Education: Conditions for Systemic Partnerships[1]

Dr. Nancy L. Zimpher, President
University of Cincinnati

Much has happened in the years since the initial warning signal of "A Nation at Risk" was sounded, including the compilation of standards for what students should know and be able to do, the attention to assessing what teacher education graduates should know and be able to do and the effort to achieve certification by veteran teachers through the National Board for Professional Teaching Standards. Now, with the comprehensive accountability effort being put forward through the Bush administration's No Child Left Behind (NCLB) agenda, accountability and teacher education meet again. David Imig, president and CEO of the American Association of Colleges for Teacher Education was recently quoted in the Washington Post as observing: "If fully enacted, these policy proposals [of the NCLB reform] would redirect existing federal support for teacher education to alternative or nontraditional providers, including local school districts, and seriously impair the capacity of education schools to prepare and support sufficient numbers of high-quality beginning teachers" (January 14, 2003, page A12). As the article notes, the Bush administration has pledged to spend $2.85 billion in coming years on alternatives to traditional teacher education, putting the onus on schools of education and universities in general to become more effective and flexible in the preparation of teachers for our nation's schools.

This attention to the redesign of university-based teacher education is not new to Washington policy makers. In the fall of 1999, former U.S. Department of Education Secretary Richard Riley convened more than 100 university presidents to impress upon them the all-university interest in the education of teachers. Bemoaning the results of a 1999 report on teacher quality, Riley observed that universities should do a better job of preparing prospective teachers, particularly in the subjects they plan to teach, and further evoked that "the entire university ought to be involved in the college of education." When teachers fail, Riley admonished, "it's not the teacher's fault;

1Adopted from remarks delivered at Taking the Lead: A Deans Summit on Education for a Technological World, The Institute of Electrical and Electronics Engineers, Inc., Baltimore, MD, Oct. 1-2, 2001.

it's the university's fault." Vartan Gregorian (1996) now head of the esteemed Carnegie Corporation of New York, once observed that universities that have schools of education "...should place them in the intellectual mainstream of the university, or else shut them down." In short, he adds, "schools of education should not be isolated, degraded, apologized for; rather, the central mission of any university ought to be ...to educate a new generation of citizens."

Schools of education must reform themselves from the inside out. While this is a necessary step in enhancing teaching and learning, it is not sufficient. A much broader base of ownership must be apparent in institutions that truly commit themselves to improving the quality of the teachers we graduate. Further, school systems and other key community constituencies must be engaged as full partners in our efforts to improve the quality of teaching. To realize the complex nature of these school/university relationships, three issues remain central to the partnership equation. First, do all the parties recognize the powerful connection between good teaching and good learning? And, if so, why is it still so challenging to accept the centrality of quality teaching to learner success? Further, how can we place this powerful connection at the center of our partnership efforts to reform teacher education? Hopefully the following summary attends to these issues as the bedrock of effective school/university partnerships for the redesign of teacher education.

Expertise in teaching is still shrouded in the myths or commonplace assumptions about the act of teaching. Some still believe that good teaching is a function of the genes; that is, that women are gender-bound to teach and teach well, a profession based mainly on nurturing capacities. Others believe that good teaching is a function of the literally thousands of hours logged in just watching other teachers. Consequently, good teaching when delivered masterfully has the uncanny effect of making teaching look "easy;" the result being, "I can do that!" Still others, often those who teach the disciplines, ascribe to the mantra, "show me someone who knows her discipline, and I'll show you a good teacher!" This assumption rests on the notion that there is no science of pedagogy, only the science of the discipline.

Veteran teachers provide another view, often characterized as OJT—on-the-job training. In other words, as teachers mature, they tend to believe that everything they know about teaching stems only from their experiences in real, live classrooms; universities represent a theoretical view of teaching that no longer rings true to their experienced perspective. And universities add complication to complexity by denying the relevance of pedagogy to the curriculum of the doctoral program, choosing instead to focus the prospective professorate's training largely on issues of research methodology. This of course misses the point that most Ph.D.s are headed for institutions where the teaching load far exceeds opportunities or expectations to conduct research. In short, commonplace assumptions about teaching tend to deny "the scientific basis of the art of teaching," making the science of teaching everybody's yet nobody's work.

Juxtapose these assumptions to increasingly substantiated evidence that clearly links teacher quality to learner outcomes. Here I refer to studies initially conducted by University of Tennessee researchers William L. Sanders and June C. Rivers, and subsequently replicated in other large urban school districts, wherein students with repeated access to high quality teachers considerably outperform students consistently exposed to less competent teachers. This kind of research design is called a "within subjects" design, where each pupil serves as her or his own point of comparison. Further, according to the careful analysis offered by Carnegie Corporation Vice President Dan Fallon at the U.S. Secretary of Education's 1999 Conference on Teacher Quality, "this kind of research also controls for all the variables unique to pupils, such as their intrinsic motivation, their work habits, the influence of their parents, and their socioeconomic status. The only variable that can explain this outcome is the quality of the teacher." Thus, while there continues to be much denial about the soundness of content-specific pedagogical understandings as a necessary ingredient in teacher preparation, evidence to the contrary serves to underscore the importance of colleges of the arts, sciences and humanities working collaboratively with their education colleagues to produce high-quality teachers.

This brings us squarely to the issue at hand: What is our role in recruiting, preparing and supporting the continuing professional development of teachers, and as importantly, what is at the core of quality teaching? Some things we know. The effects of teacher preparation must be felt at all levels of the continuum of teaching: who we recruit to teaching, what pre-professional and professional experiences temper their process of "learning to teach," who and how we are engaged in the critical early years of teaching, and what are the most effective learning experiences for veteran teachers. Here are three axioms that should guide our thinking:

1. Good learning is a function of good teaching.

2. Good teaching is a function of good teacher education.

3. Good teacher education is a function of a seamless and interactive relationship between educators in the disciplines (i.e., arts, sciences and humanities) with those in pedagogical studies and those who teach in elementary and secondary schools.

The remainder of this discussion focuses on what's to be gained by a university partnership between teacher educators and faculty who teach in the disciplines, and the linkage of that collaboration to partnership with elementary and secondary education school systems. To this end, I will briefly share a set of conditions that could guide cooperative university partnerships across academic units, and school-university partnerships that could more effectively link higher education with K-12 education.

Condition No. 1: A Shared Conception of Teaching and Learning. The "charm of teacher education" (Clark 1985) characterizes the field as "...easily accessible in every sense of that term: geographically proximate to the consumer, easy to enter, short in duration, optimally convenient to the remainder of the college student's academic program, easy to complete, inexpensive, non-exclusive (i.e., does not rule out other career options), etc." In short, teacher education programs are rarely "conceptually coherent;" that is, designed to reflect common understandings among program designers (let alone, schools that subsequently employ candidates) of what teachers should know and be able to do. In the best case, programs would reflect a shared conception of good teaching so clearly understood by all participants that teacher graduates, cooperating teachers, professors and school hiring officials would be able to recognize these qualities in the graduates they hire. [See Standards from the National Council for Accreditation of Teacher Education for more on this topic.]

Compelling examples of conceptual coherence are documented in case studies conducted more than a decade ago (Howey & Zimpher 1987). Specifically, the design initiatives for contrasting conceptions of teaching at Michigan State University include, for example, a discipline based pedagogy in the "academic learning" program and commitments to cultural competence and diversity in the "heterogeneous classrooms" program. More contemporary program conceptions include Donald Schön's (1983; 1987; 1991) framework for "teacher as reflective practitioner" and Yinger's (1992) use of the architectural construct of "patterned language" in the design of the University of Cincinnati teacher education program.

Condition No. 2: The Continuum of Teacher Development. This step introduces the concept of "learning to teach." Already a case has been made for the scientific bases for the art of teaching. Here we add the notion that these acquired learnings take into account that the process of learning to teach is developmental in nature. The continuum begins as students decide to pursue teaching as a career and continues through pre-professional and professional teacher education through the induction phase or beginning years of teaching, and throughout the maturing teacher's lifetime career. To this point, Susan Rosenholtz's (1989) work on the developmental nature of teaching asked teachers in high performing, learning-enriched schools and low performing, learning-impoverished schools to reflect on the question, "how long does it take to learn to teach?" - resulting in the following observations:

Learning-impoverished schools: I learned by my third year. How to handle kids so they pay attention, what you're going to teach them and how, takes a little time. You also need to be familiar with the textbooks you use. Without them you'd be lost. I'd say two years. The first year you're so nervous and everything is so new. You're trying to shuffle through the new paperwork, all the new books, feeling your way. The second year you start to relax, and you really start to teach. I think that after that second year you have the confidence that you know how to teach.

Learning enriched schools: You always keep learning. You never stop. Every child is different and a challenge, so you have to keep learning in order to help each one. We have upper middle and lower SES students in our school. That makes a very wide range. We need different ways to deal with those differences in background.

I think it takes your whole career, really. Even today, I may find a great idea or even another teacher may use a great idea, and it may not work for me. If it doesn't work, then I'm going to try something else. Different students respond to different things. What works wonderfully for one child may not with another. There is no recipe for good teaching.

Obviously, teachers who appreciate the complexities of teaching and the developmental nature of teaching are, in fact, more likely to be found and found in greater numbers in highly successful schools.

Condition No. 3: All-University Means Pre-professional Education Too. The early years of teacher preparation are typically perceived, by many students who engage in general liberal studies, as a "pass through" phenomena; that is, how quickly and painlessly can "I" get these general studies requirements under my belt? Often courses are selected based on the time of day offered, or the reputation of the instructor, and not for the intrinsic values of truly becoming liberally educated–a prerequisite to good teaching, no matter what the discipline or grade level. Colleagues in arts, sciences and humanities and education must effectively frame a set of foundational courses along with their colleagues in the arts and sciences that will broaden the intellectual horizons of prospective teachers and at the same time build an important intellectual foundation for appreciation of diversity and cultural competence. [See Brown, Jay (2003) and www.uwm.edu/MilwaukeeIdea/.]

Condition No. 4: Teacher Recruitment. Referencing curriculum that emphasizes culture suggests that we must also be committed to the challenge of recruiting a high-quality and diverse cohort of prospective students into careers in teaching. Candidates for careers in teaching are in our midst daily, but still most teacher candidates represent a highly homogenous cadre of middle class, Anglo females who travel less than 100 miles away from home to attend college, and who aspire to teach in settings close to home. These candidates are often monolingual and exude a cultural myopia not reflective of the modern day diverse classroom that characterizes urban, and increasingly suburban and small town education, where the demand for teaching is the most intense. Our collective goal should be to recruit more high-performing students into teaching, and especially from cultural and ethnic backgrounds more reflective of urban society and our global context (RATE VII 1994)

Condition No. 5: Integration of Disciplinary Knowledge with Pedagogy. Too often our deliberations about teaching and learning hinge on the "tyranny of the OR"; that is, good teachers either know their discipline or know pedagogy. On the contrary, we need improved techniques for enabling prospective teachers to better integrate disciplinary knowledge with pedagogical knowledge. One vehicle for such would be to offer a sequence of courses wherein professors co-design and co-deliver such courses involving, on a selective basis, teachers from elementary and secondary contexts as well. At the very least, forming integrated disciplinary teams across colleges of arts, sciences and humanities and education would be a start in the right direction.

Condition No. 6: Professional Development Schools and New Roles and Responsibilities. While integration of the teaching discipline with pedagogical understandings is an important factor in program design, the integration of didactic, on-campus course experiences with campus and school-based laboratory experiences is yet another imperative of our partnership. The most pervasive analogue is found in medical education. Since the depression-era Flexner Report, it has been simply understood that medical education must increasingly be both research-based and experientially based. Thus came the beginnings of the concept of the "teaching hospital," and no prominent medical education program exists today without one. But field experiences in teacher education have been riddled with deficiencies for years: inadequate selection and oversight of assignments, ill-prepared and rarely involved veteran teachers who understand the program and the import of the field experiences, and few attempts on campus to create video laboratories or Internet connections with live teaching sites in local schools. Campuses must step forward to create intensive laboratory experiences as testing sites for the intellectual and applied dimensions of their programs.

The integration of campus didactic, laboratory and field experiences suggests that schools and universities need to revisit the roles and responsibilities of university faculty and K-12 teachers toward the creation of "clinical faculty," not unlike the designation of some in the health professions. At UWM, we are experimenting with the concept of "teachers-in-residence." Public school teachers are released for two years to spend time both on campus and in the school district to help actualize the kinds of reforms discussed herein. [See Zimpher 2002.]

Condition No. 7: Cross-role Preparation and the Formation of Interdisciplinary Teams. Just as increasing demands are placed on teaching schools, called Professional Development Schools (Tomorrow's Schools 1990), to assist in improved preparation of teachers, so also must the sites consider the relationship between the preparation of teachers and other professionals who serve schools, like principals, guidance counselors, art specialists, and those involved in physical education and coaching.

No less important than cross-role training to teacher preparation is the interdisciplinary nature of schools. High schools, especially, are no less segregated by discipline than are higher education institutions, so it ought to be no wonder that high schools are as challenged to integrate the disciplines as are we in higher education. Designing block curriculum and streams of content integration both in engineering, the arts and sciences, and in education would go a long way to enable prospective teachers to gain appreciation for the value added by interdisciplinary studies, and hopefully provide a model for high school and middle school integration concurrently.

Condition No. 8: PDSs as Places Where Teachers Keep on Learning. So long as the concept of a "teaching school" or Professional Development School is gaining in popularity and recognition as a vital element of teacher preparation, it should also be understood that these sites are models of adult learning as well as demonstration sites for student learning. So why not create in the PDS a profound respect for the importance of teacher growth and development as well as a student learner-centered school? Schools that value teacher learning would readily display announcements for professional development opportunities, certificates of accomplishment by teachers as well as students, and create spaces reserved for teacher learning and study, just like for students. Professional teachers should also be afforded special recognition within the academy through special titles, like "clinical faculty" or the designation used at UWM, "teacher in residence." Accordingly, professors who participate in schools should carry special designation as contributors to the learning environment of that school. Yet, for now, the "hustle and bustle" of contemporary life for teachers leaves little time for professional consultation and reflection. Witness this hypothetical "want ad," contrived by Linda Darling-Hammond for the 1996 National Commission on Teaching & America's Future Report:

WANTED

> College graduate with academic major (master's degree preferred). Excellent communication/leadership skills required. Challenging opportunity to serve 150 clients daily on a tight schedule, developing up to five different products each day to meet individual needs, while adhering to multiple product specifications. Adaptability helpful, since suppliers cannot always deliver goods on time, incumbent must arrange for own support services, and customers rarely know what they want. Ideal candidate will enjoy working in isolation from colleagues. This diversified position allows employee to exercise typing, clerical, law enforcement, and social work skills between assignments and after hours. Typical workweek: 50 hours. Special nature of work precludes amenities such as telephones or computers, but work has many intrinsic rewards. Starting salary $24,661, rising to $36,495 after only 15 years. (p. 54)

Condition No. 9: Institutional Changes. Schools are said to be hidebound, controlled by the imperatives of the lunch hour ("the banana"), the clock ("the bell"), transportation problems ("the bus") and infrastructure issues like access to the school depending on when the janitor unlocks the doors ("the broom"). In similarly alliterative fashion, universities are controlled by the institutional imperatives of "term, traffic, tenure, etc." But education any time, any place, or just-in-time delivery of instruction are changing higher education and elementary and secondary education. So we have to see our role in the education of teachers as preparing for these new and novel learning environments, beginning with creating more flexibility in the way we design and deliver our programs, and encouraging our school partners to do the same.

The greatest challenge that we face in achieving quality teaching is our own institutional separatism. Schools of education prepare teachers, often without interaction or engagement with those in the arts and sciences who offer foundational knowledge and the teaching major in engineering and/or arts and sciences. When veteran expert teachers are engaged in teacher preparation, they are often active only at the school site, not in the design and development of the entire teacher education program. When faculty members serve in supervisory roles in schools, they are not regular participants in school planning, curriculum development or teaching on site. Hiring policies still constrain conditions for beginning teachers and if peer assistance programs are in place, they rarely link conditions and expectations promoted in the teacher education programs to conditions and expectations in the early years of teaching. Colleges and universities offer continuing education courses whether they fit the curricular needs of the schools from which their enrollees come. In short, each of us takes some responsibility for some component of the continuum, but there has not been an effective way to bridge those components so that we have a common, some say, aligned system like the more established professions (of law, medicine, business – and the health professions) for achieving teacher quality.

Further, echoing the challenges put forward by former Secretary of Education Riley and Carnegie CEO Gregorian, university presidents must take their rightful place in encouraging reforms in teacher preparation, alongside their K-12 colleagues, the district superintendent, union leader and board chair, and their deans of education, arts, sciences and humanities. Efforts to form operative P-16 councils, like our Milwaukee Partnership Academy, provide the forum for enabling change and removing institutional barriers that impede programs.

Condition No. 10: A Redesign Model. Several years ago, physicist Ken Wilson published Redesigning Education (1994) in which he challenges educators to create redesign models as discoveries and educational breakthroughs begin to change our practices and our understandings of the consequences of education. We have no such redesign models. The little red schoolhouse still rules and insights about educational innovation are still not well documented. Thus, we are obliged to study the changes we are making in our programming, assess the consequences of these changes, benchmark them against best practices elsewhere, toward the redesign of educational practice.

Conclusion

Ending where we began, the "common places of education" must give way to emerging empirical evidence that quality teaching matters in the learning lives of America's youth. The imperative of the National Commission on Teaching and America's Future (1996) compelled us to place a competent, caring and qualified teacher in every child's classroom by 2006 (NCTAF, 1996:4). In a time of the greatest turnover of teachers in our nation's history, the opportunity to truly enable quality teaching is finally a real possibility. Lee Iacocca said it best, "In a truly rational society, the best of us would be teachers, and the rest would have to settle for something less."

References

Brown, Thomas, Gregory Jay and Darrell Rerrell. (2002). "Planting a New Kind of Teacher: The Cultures and Communities/MPS Experiment," *Metropolitan Universities: An International Forum* (Partnerships for Urban Teacher Education). IUPUI.

Gregorian, Vartan. (1996). "The University and School History Education," Available from: http://63.70.163.70/nche/archives/may_news.html.

Howey, K. and Nancy Zimpher. (1987)."The Role of Higher Education in Initial Year of Teaching Programs," In Griffin and Millies (eds.), *The First Year of Teaching: Background Papers and a Proposal.* IL: Illinois State Board of Education.

RATE VII – Teaching Teachers: Facts & Figures (Teacher Preparation in the Urban Context), (1994). AACTE.

Rosenholtz, Susan. (1989).*Teacher's Workplace: The Social Organization of Schools*, New York: Longman.

Sanders, William and June Rivers. (1996). "Cumulative and Residual Effects of Teachers on Future Student Academic Achievement," Value-Added Research and Assessment Center, University of Tennessee, Knoxville, TN.

Schon, Donald. *The Reflective Practitioner: How Professionals Think in Action*, (1983.) New York: Basic Books.

______. *Educating the Reflective Practitioner: Toward a New design for Teaching and Learning in the Professions*, (1987.) San Francisco: Jossey-Bass.

______. *The Reflective Turn: Case Studies in and on Educational Practice*, (1991.) New York: Teachers Press, Columbia University.

Tomorrow's Schools: Principles for the Design of Professional Development Schools, (1990.) The Holmes Group.

What Matters Most: Teaching for America's Future, (1996.) Report of the National Commission on Teaching and America's Future.

Wilson, Ken and Bennett Davis. (1994.) *Redesigning Education*, New York: Henry Holt.

Yinger, R.J. and Hendricks-Lee. (1992.) "A Pattern Language for Teachers," *Journal of Teacher Education*. 43:5. 367-375.

Zimpher, Nancy. "Partnering for Systemic Change," (2002.) *Metropolitan Universities: An International Forum* (Partnerships for Urban Teacher Education). IUPUI.

Developing Leaders: The Greatest Challenge for Education Reform

Dr. Vermelle Johnson
Past Sr. V.P. and V.P. for Academic Affairs
Claflin University
and
Member of the Board, S.C.
Commission on Higher Education

Until we are able to produce leaders who can view the entire education spectrum and bring to the planning table ideas beyond personal opinion and void of politics, the call for education reform will continue to be a "tinkling symbol," signifying very little.

Until we are able to produce leaders who can help us refocus our commitment to public education, while indeed creating some choices along the way, the call for education reform will become rhetorical in its messages and insincere in its meaning.

Until we are able to produce leaders who understand the interplay of "revolution" vs. "evolution" as we draw up strategic plans for the future, we will continue to create a system that is long on change but short on reform.

The Landscape

Restructure, Reorganize, Remake, Reinvent! These are but a few of the expressions that tell tales of frenzy, of scrambling, of apprehension and, fortunately, of some serious attempts to move forward in improving almost every sector of our existence. Education is no exception. Education, the sector that is most germane to any progress that we will make as a nation, is taking a lion's share of inconstancy as we attempt to "reform," The law is clear, "reform or suffer the consequences of being labeled impaired."

The Mandate

The current climate of uncertainty faced by classroom teachers and educators across the nation is rooted, in part, in the year-old "No Child Left Behind" federal mandate, signed into law by the President in January, 2002. This law, while it has the power of a partial "wake-up" call, has the longer-term potential of nudging educational leadership in each state to enact stricter accountability standards in moving education forward. However, the law, itself, sets unrealistic standards in its proficiency requirements; thus, the need for serious planning and leadership ahead. The federal government, in its attempt to become more significantly involved in "fixing" the nation's public schools, has at the same time sent mixed messages as to how this is to be accomplished.

Among other things, the new law compels each state to increase education standards and put into place rigorous expectations for progressive achievement over the next twelve years. All students must be proficient in their scores on identified tests – all schools must be 100% proficient. There are new competency requirements for classroom teachers and teachers' aides. The federal government will issue new standards to indicate how much progress a school should make each year.

If a school fails to "measure up," parents of that school will have the option of enrolling their child/children in better performing schools.

The Confusion

While, on the surface, the No Child Left Behind law would seem to focus the country in the direction of improving education, nationally, there are currents of confusion that, if not dealt with quickly in a sensible and futuristic thinking manner, will impede the very progress the law is meant to create. Some veteran teachers, for instance, view the new requirements for teachers and teachers' aides as an insult, in that they believe that they are forever having to prove their worth, no matter how excellent their past performance. Dealing swiftly and sanely with this potentially morale-boggling problem is essential. Chief among the questions being raised by educators, however, is "What is proficient?" Is it realistic to believe that all children will be able to attain a "B," the level generally accepted as proficient? The fact that we give parents the option to move away from a "poor performing" school could wreak havoc on the morale and psychological well-being of those who remain. This option, if carried out to any significant extent, would seem to fly in the face of No Child Left Behind. The remaining children could very well be "left behind" forever.

A Partial Solution

We must bring in and listen to some "new voices," those who are closest to the problems of reform, and give them an opportunity to share some basics that are totally foreign to most of today's so-called "experts" in education.

As indicated by the title of this presentation, we must build leaders – strong, competent, confident – to deal with these compelling, yet sensitive, problems. And, if we would hope to accomplish any measurable degree of success in true education reform, these leaders must represent the total population—leaving no pool of talent untapped. In South Carolina, according to a report by the Institute for Women's Policy Research, the utilization of women in decision-making lags woefully behind the rest of the nation. While women in the state are more likely than women in most states to work as managers or professionals, they are the worst in the nation for their proportion among legislative officials. Thus, they have little or no impact on policy or decision-making, which includes, among other things, the direction of education. Examination of these phenomena indicates that, on the surface, it's a "cultural thing."

A closer look at the educational landscape of the local tri-county area of mid-state South Carolina (Orangeburg, Calhoun, and Bamberg) reveals that, like the state as a whole, women are being assigned top-level education management positions in record numbers. They are doing outstanding jobs in carrying out mandates that they, themselves, had little or no input in enacting and for which they have received too little direct preparation for smoother handling of the inherent problems they face. They don't complain - they just get the job done. It seems indeed a "cultural thing."

Out of the urgent need to begin to build leadership among women, Project GEMS, LDP, (Girls Emulating Maturity and Strength, a Leadership Development Program) was born. To change the culture in South Carolina is to open up a vast arena of talent, women's talent that is vital to the progress of the state, to education reform. Women should not only be expected to share significantly in setting policy and decision making, but they should also see it as their responsibility to do so.

GEMS, LDP, is an initiative that has established a tri-level mentoring network to include high school girls from Orangeburg-Wilkinson (Rhinestones), college coeds from Claflin University (Diamonds-in-the-Rough), and women professionals from diverse leadership positions (Diamonds). Through a series of strategically designed coursework, seminars, round-tables, symposia, and other activities, these girls and women collaborate to promote the professional development of young women who aspire to achieve at the highest level of leadership within their chosen professions. Similar to but unlike a popular South Carolina initiative, "Call Me Mister," that focuses on preparing young men for the elementary classroom, GEMS, LDP, often uses a motto that says Call Me Ph.D., Principal, Superintendent, Dean, Scientist, CEO, President.

Having received start-up funding through the generosity of the Sunshine Lady Foundation, Inc. and through the local Teacher Quality Enhancement

Partnership Grant (US Department of Education), GEMS, Ltd. was fully implemented in the Fall of 2002, with a second university in lower South Carolina committed to begin the program in Fall 2003. Pending funding, at least five programs will be fully implemented by Fall 2006.

Beyond the experience and structured training that girls of GEMS will receive as they prepare for roles of leadership, the program has spawned the pursuit of a much bigger, more comprehensive initiative, A South Carolina Center for Women's Professional Development. In addition to the goal espoused by GEMS, the Center, of which GEMS is a major part, would have three additional goals (briefly stated):

1. To create a research and advocacy society to identify problems faced directly by women as they aspire to roles of leadership.
2. To assist communities in addressing some so-called "little problems" that have far-reaching impacts in shaping the cultural atmosphere that affect the way women live and the way girls are raised.
3. To provide structured in-service training and programs for women in professional leadership/management positions.

In all of the above, the major aim (for women and men) is that of enhancing competence and confidence, building self-esteem, promoting enthusiasm, renewing vigor and determination, and creating an environment conducive to growth. The groundwork has been laid and a significant number of colleges and universities have committed to lead the way. Pending funding, the goal is to have each institution of higher education in the state intricately involved in this effort.

As we attempt to reform education across the country, South Carolina can, and if funded, will make very significant progress through the Center for Women's Professional Development, in fixing the cultural things that will sustain short-term change, aimed at long-term education reform.

Behind the School Stood the Community in Collaborative Partnership

Dr. Bettie Hicks, Mrs. Nancy Ford, Dr. Helen Brantley

Dr. Helen Brantley, Professor
South Carolina State University

Dr. Bettie Hicks, Principal
Whittaker Elementary School
and
Mrs. Nancy Ford
Orangeburg Consolidated District Five

Bridging the Achievement Gap: Collaborative Efforts Among PK12 Schools, Universities and Diverse Communities

The article describes the development of a collaborative model designed to "Bridge the Achievement Gap" based on environments that encourage change and promote high quality of learning and instruction. The article describes instances and types of relevant experiences required to facilitate internal and external collaboration among supported communities. The concept of alignment is used to emphasize interconnectedness among the stakeholders as they engender intellectually creative and socially important synergy in their potential to generate needed solutions to the achievement gap. Systematic and consistent alignment of learners in an inseparable web of long-term supported relationships is a suggested strategy for working cohesively in creating greater community and student success.

There is compelling research that emphasizes the wide disparity between the achievement of public school students. It indicates a very clear message that there is a serious achievement gap between minority and non-minority students, especially in poor rural and urban areas. In the days of accountability, it is quite explicit that the gap-is apparently getting worse and has future implications in the areas of successful educational, productive employment, and economic growth, (Johnson & Viadero 2000). This wide disparity in predicted educational and economic outcomes between America's minority and non-minority populations has contributed to the achievement gap phenomenon. The gap is so pervasive, it can be seen in communities, schools, classrooms and higher educational programs for the training of teachers. It impacts grades, test scores, dropout rates, college entrances rates, teacher in-training college completion rate and first year job success rate, and parental school involvement rate, (Blair 2000; Education Week 1999; Gordon 2000; King 1999; Simmons 1999; Orlans 1999; Viadero 2000; The College Board, 1999; Education USA 2000).

Equally important, are the research studies that continually emphasize teachers' attitudes and dispositions toward poor achieving minority students in rural schools or urban depressed areas. For instance, Ferguson's extensive meta-analysis (1998) reveals that teachers, both black and white, almost always have lower expectations for African-American students than they do for white students. Arroyo, Road and Drew (1999) as well as The College Board (1999) researched a similar conclusion and go on to note that this way of behaving has an impact on the self-esteem and self-concept of minority students. Thus, the low self-expectations, coupled with teachers' low expectations of them, lead to low performance and achievement.

Caldas and Bankston (1997; 1998) see this situation and its negative effects on achievement as being even more prevalent in schools where the culture is one of mediocrity, tracking of students, and where minority students are poor and under achieving. Tracking of students for instructional purposes also lends itself to the achievement gap. Conversely, it seems that everyone's expectation level rise in schools with mixed populations, as does minority achievement. In fact, in schools where the non-minority students outnumber the minority students, the achievement gap is typically narrower. The achievement gap also tends to be narrower in schools that use mixed-ability rather than homogeneous grouping strategies, even in schools that have high-minority, high-poverty populations, (Roscigno 1998; Viadero, 2000).

There is a need to collaborate and problem solve on a regular basis to narrow the gap. A collaborative climate that promotes *high quality of learning and instruction, supported by best practices and alignment among quality learning, instruction, competent teachers, and higher education working as a collaborative community is plausible!*

Aligning Standards for High Quality Learning and Instruction

Academically rigorous curriculum creates a school culture of "serious business." The instructional climate becomes one of high quality learning and producing for everyone in the school environment, teachers, administrators, parents, community and students. The tone and flare that sends the message that: "High quality Learning and Instruction Take Place Here." a high quality and learning environment possess sends a clear and compelling message that indicates without a doubt *"achievement must take place here."* This kind of environment focuses on the strengths of students and utilizes a variety of strategies at different levels of learning and instruction. Factors must be in place designed to move student to the next level of "knowing" in order that the optimal growth/learning occurs.

Several Studies have indicated that students who were exposed to "high quality" instruction learned more than students who did not receive such instruction (Brophy & Good, 1986; Stevenson & Stigler, 1992; Wang, 1998). In schools where high quality instruction is taking place, the environment is one of interactive learning and high expectations. Students are at the centered of the learning process and have an active role during instruction. The school is receptive to new ideas and experimentation of methods and strategies.

Aligning the Most Effective Teachers to the Lowest Performing Students

If teachers demonstrate interest in diverse ideas and culture, it is much more likely that students in diverse settings will flourish during learning. All teachers must be trained on techniques for best reaching the instructional and learning potential of racial, ethnic, cultural, and socio-economically diverse students and their families, (Garrett, 2002). When the curriculum is relevant of high quality (not just memorizations of skills) coupled with competent teachers, than students are stimulated to learn.

In the *School Achievement Structure Study* (1998), administrators carefully selected teachers who possessed the disposition to make a difference in the classroom. Other teachers (focused teachers) with less ability to carry out the subject matter in diverse settings were provided with on-going modeling and regular professional development.

Student-centered instructional classrooms were emphasized by the principal who aligned the best teachers to work with students in stannines of "4" and below on content skills and concepts. Additionally, small work groups of students, manipulative, and computer-based activities were emphasized throughout the work sessions.

Aligning University to Low Performing Schools Enhances Teaching

Schools of Education must be driven to seek out low performing schools and students to provide "best practices" aligned to student characteristics. Schools of Education must also prepare pre-service teachers for the 21st century classroom, (an array of students from a variety of cultural backgrounds (Morgan, 2002). Further, accreditation and professional bodies are advocating that curriculum, field experiences, and clinical practice help candidates to demonstrate knowledge, skills, and dispositions related to diversity, (NCATE, 2002). Low performing schools can provide the ideal diverse settings for Preservice teachers to gain the necessary skills to teach all students to learn. In a variety of diverse settings, they can examine their beliefs about teaching, apply humanistic practices and acquire the knowledge, skills and dispositions to become competent beginning teachers. Such milieu can also enhance professional practice in all content areas through collaborative reflection, inquiry and modeling. Pre-service teachers, in-service teachers and college professors working collaboratively are able to create class settings conducive to greater student achievement. As college professors and in-service teachers model strategies, approaches and content in challenging, explicit, and compelling way, pre-service teachers expand their knowledge about subject matter, student learning and various styles of teaching.

Solutions to the Achievement Gap

Using standards will help schools to prepare students and teacher education candidates with the preparation of quality instruction that helps students to go beyond rote memory and regurgitation. Connecting to student's background knowledge, prior experience, verbal, and non-verbal exposure. Capturing experiences where students appreciate the connection by actively and joyfully participating in class activities. The following scenario provides an example:

One of the authors recently observed a teacher during a lesson of a story was entitled, "The secret life of a seal." This is a third grade story with its setting in Alaska. The teacher knowing that her students could not connect to the story directly assisted them with lots of illustrations, personal connections, artifacts and music from the Alaskan culture. Her class composition included the following: 4 students with special needs, 1 classified as gifted and learning disabled, 13 below average performer and 7 average performers. The teacher pre-assessed her students at the beginning of the school year using multiple forms of assessments including an interest inventory. Through the process, she gained insights into variations in learning styles.

Utilizing this information for instructional purposes, she prepared daily activities for her students. Research (Melton, Pickett & Sherer, and (1999) shows that teachers should link instruction to all the learning styles/multiple intelligences of students during a lesson.

The teacher, then discussed pre-story concepts such as brave, strong courage, helpful, caring and had her students to connect through character education as they shared their meaning of words, provided examples and illustrations of the term. In addition to the discussion, students were asked to represent the terms through, writing, drawing, discussing and acting out their perceptions of each term. As they shared, the teacher treated students with respect, acceptance and equity as she created a class climate of teaching, learning and sharing.

> *Teacher: How many people wear coats in the winter? (All of the students raised their hands)*
>
> *Teacher: what are some of the reasons you would wear a coat?*
>
> *Students: To keep warm, to feel warm, to put something on your body, to protect your heart from the wind, so the wind will not make you cold. So that your body does not freeze. So your head does not get cold.*
>
> *Teacher: How many students have coats with hoods on them? Many students raised their hands. "Well, in Alaska, students wear coats just as you do for the same reasons you have mentioned," she said, "Their coats are called Parkas." She wrote the word on the overhead next to the word coat, and showed them a picture of a child from the Alaskan culture wearing one standing next to his Alaskan Husky. She asked questions about the picture on the cover of the book. She also asked questions such as, "Why do you think the boy is holding his dog? What role does the dog play in his life?" Again, she engaged students in a real-life task by asking, "Do you know of a situation where dogs help others?" After students gave a multiplicity of responses, one student said, "My uncle has a dog to help him cross the street, go shopping, attend church and travels with him wherever he goes. He even brings him to my house when he comes; you know, he's blind," the student said. The teacher was very patient as the other students then asked questions of the students who provided that response. As she looked from student to student they discussed and asked questions of the boy who told of his uncle's condition and the relationship of the dog in his life. The teacher than, connected the role of the dog the student shared to the role of the dogs in lives of the Alaskan. One student raised her hand and asked, "Are you going to read the story to us?"*

Research shows that culturally relevant teaching refers to methods of teaching that empower students to grown intellectually, socially, and emotionally by using cultural referents in teaching knowledge and skills (Harmon & Pang, 2001). The teacher related content to students' background, experiences and exposure. She used examples and illustrations from their culture to connect to the story.

How can school build the necessary school culture to build quality pedagogy that enhances quality learning and instruction? What are the characteristics of school culture that extends students' prior knowledge, experience and exposure to worlds beyond their immediate area without leaving the classroom? What are characteristics of school culture that encourages diversity and acceptance in all students irrespective of their SES, class cultural and achievement?

Building the Collaborative Community

There is a need to collaborate and problem solve on a regular basis to narrow the achievement gap. Creative solutions and human resources enhance quality learning and instruction. When the mission of the school is "student achievement," then you find all constituents in the organization working toward the good of the mission. Research demonstrates that collaboration in schools can have significant effects on student achievement in reading, mathematics and social studies (Newmann and Wehlage 1995). The results of a School Restructuring Study (SRS) of 24 elementary, middle, and high schools promote the idea of a collaborative community. The study demonstrates significant gains in academic subjects as much as 31 percentile points. In the School Achievement Structure Study (2001), the emphasis also, speaks to the need of an organizational structure of collaboration (parents, community businesses, universities, community groups and) to elevate student learning and achievement. Collegiality, high quality instruction, professional development, modeling, frequent monitoring of class instruction, aligning to the standards, instructional resources, frequent performance based assessment and class size reduction contributed to academic learning and achievement of students. The School Achievement Structure Study utilized ten-routines, in addition to qualitative and quantitative class assessment aligned to standards. Thus, several high schools and elementary schools were removed from probationary status in the Chicago School System as a result of the effects of the Structured Ten Routines (Sizemore, 1994, 1998, 2000, 2001).

Student performance is increased when the ultimate goal of the collaborative community partnership is to elevate achievement in PK-12 students. This mission must permeate all settings and fabric of the collaborative community. The collaboration should occur in churches, community centers, in a variety of meetings, teams, centers of concerned citizens and places and institutions of learning. In a collaboration of university, public schools, parents, and students, there are opportunities for growth for all involved as they contribute collectively to the purpose: achievement of students. Through collective work and responsibility, achievement becomes the norm.

Where school buildings, grade-point averages and standardized test scores are demonstrating bleak pictures, teacher education programs should be mandated to prepare teacher candidates who can make a difference through planning for instruction, instructional delivery, appropriate assessment, technology and the right disposition to provide meaningful learning experiences for diverse students in a variety of settings. Additionally, teacher education candidates must work effectively with families, communities, colleagues, agencies, and other groups in meaningful ways to optimize learning for all students. Then we can truly say, "Behind the school stood the community in collaborative partnership" with synergy that elevates each and every one to new learning and professional growth in renaissance of commitment and responsibility. (Brantley, 1995 and 2000)

References

Johnson, R., & D. Viadero. (2000). Unmet Promise: Raising Minority Achievement. *Education Week* (March 15, 2000). Online: www.edweek.org.

Brantley, H. (2000). A Collaborative Partnership: PreSTEP/Service Learning. South Carolina State University, Teacher Quality Enhancement

Brantley, H. (1995). Higher Level of Thinking in Rural Students: A Comprehensive Study. U. S. Department of Agriculture, under Project No. SCX-206-05-87, South Carolina State University

Arroyo, A., R. Rhoad, & P. Drew. (1999). Meeting Diverse Student Needs in Urban Schools: Research-Based Recommendations for School Personnel.: Preventing School Failure Vol. 43, No. 4: 145-153.

Blair, J. (2000). Minorities post gains in higher ed., but still trail whites. *Education Week* (February 16, 2000). Online: www.edweek.org.

Brantley, H. (1998). Crane is on the move with the ten routines. In The Process - School Achievement Structure. Vol. 4, Issue 3.: p. 17.

Borman G.D. (2003). Experiments for educational evaluation and improvement. *Peabody Journal of Education*, 77(4), 7-21.

Caldas, S., & Bankston (1997). Effect of School Population Socioeconomic Status on Individual Academic Achievement. *The Journal of Educational Research* (May/June 1997): 269-276.

Caldas, S., & Bankston (1998). The Inequality of Separation: Racial Composition of Schools and Academic Achievement. *The Journal of Educational Administration Quarterly* (October 1998): 533-557.

College Board, The (1999). Reaching the Top: A Report of the National Task Force on Minority High Achievement. New York: Author.

Ferguson, R. (2000). Cultivating New Routines that Foster High Achievement for All Students: Frameworks and Ideas for Collaborating to Reduce Racial Achievement Gaps . Cambridge, MA: Harvard University, Wiener Center for Social Policy, John F. Kennedy School of Government.

Gordon, E. (2000). Bridging the New Diversity: The Minority Achievement Gap. *Principal* (May 2000).

Johnson, R., & D. Viadero. (2000). Unmet Promise: Raising Minority Achievement. *Education Week* (March 15, 2000). Online: www.edweek.org.

King, A. (1999). Closing the Education Gap: A Race Against Time. *U.S. News & World Report* (November 15, 1999).

No Child Left Behind Act 2001, Pub. L. No. 107-110, 115 Stat. 1425 (2002).

Simmons, T. (1999). Worlds Apart: The Racial Education Gap, *Raleigh News & Observer,* (December 27, 1999)

Sizemore, B, H. Brantley, K. Chase (2000). An Effective School Study: The Structured Ten Routines. *Journal of Effective Schools*

Slavin, R.R. & Madden, N.A. (2001). One Million Children: Success for All. Thousand Oaks, CA:Corwin.

Orlans, H. (1999). The Test Score Gap. Change (January 1999); 9-10.

Roscigno, V. 1(998). Race and the Reproduction of Educational Disadvantage. Social Forces (March 1998)

Viadero, D. (2000a). Even in Well-Off Suburbs, Minority Achievement Lags. *Education Week* (*March 15, 2000). Online: www. edweek.org.

Viadero, D. (2000b). Lags in Minority Achievement Defy Traditional Explanations. *Education Week* (March 22, 2000). Online: www.edweek.org.

Parental Involvement

Dr. Bernice Moore-Green
Professor of Teacher Education
South Carolina State University
and
Dr. Virginia A. Brown
Director of Instruction
Sumter School District 17

(L – R) Dr. Bernice Moore-Green, Dr. Virginia A. Brown

The parental involvement component is an important part of the South Carolina CHEC-LEA Teacher Quality Enhancement Partnership. This component is very important in that research findings support the view that parental involvement is positively related to positive student achievement, attitude toward school, motivation, self-esteem, rate of homework completion and several other variables commonly associated with success in school. Moreover, schools that have model parental involvement programs usually receive higher ratings. In addition to a review of literature, models of parental involvement and implications for teacher education programs are discussed herein.

Research documents that parental involvement and participation in the education of the child increases achievement and improves the child's positive attitude toward school. (www.ncreal.org, 2002). Parental involvement is a very wise investment strategy for learning communities as well as the civic community. Schools that recognize the importance of parental involvement are more likely to contribute to the nurturing of individuals who will make positive contributions to society and will in turn become involved parents themselves.

What the research does not provide is what kind(s) of parental involvement are the best indicators for the child's success (Baker & Soden, 1998). Though there are many ways that parents can be involved in the education of their children as well as many types of family / parental involvement, for many parents this involvement may occur only in the form of parent conferences. It follows then that schools and districts must define ways that parents can be made to feel comfortable in the school and ways that parental involvement can be made an integral part of how the school operates. (Educators Notebook On Family Involvement: Programs, Plans and Ideas, 2000). There are 30 years of research to support the fact that the most accurate predictor of a child's school success and achievement is the extent to which his parent is involved in his education (Cotton & Savard, 1982, www.nwrel.org, 2003).

Similarly, socio-economic status of the family does not matter (Comer, 1988: Chavkin & Williams, 1988). School districts, then, need to be cognizant of the areas that have been delineated as the framework of partnership between the school, home and community.

Joyce Epstein's work at Johns Hopkins University has produced a large amount of research in the area of parent involvement that is applicable to school districts with particular reference to those elements that encompass parent involvement. According to Epstein (1995), there are six types of parent involvement that schools can use to promote family involvement. Ultimately, professionals who use these tenets will realize the linkage between parent involvement and student success even without knowledge of the vast body of research. The tenets are Parenting, Communication, Volunteering, Learning at Home, Decision-making, and Collaboration with the Community. The National PTA has chosen to call these categories "The National Standards for Parent / Family Involvement Programs".

Nationally there is broad-based support for parent and family involvement. An organization such as the National PTA supports a pro-active approach, suggest that schools develop a Parent/Family Involvement Policy and National Standards for that involvement from which schools can base model programs have been created (National Standards for Parent / Family Involvement Programs, National PTA, 1998). The recent No Child Left Behind legislation (formerly the ESEA Act) places emphasis on parental involvement and provides funds for programs that are designed to increase that involvement (P. L. 107-110, Section 5131). Title I of that act requires the development of school- parent compacts that link the family to the high performance of students. National Goals 2000 legislation, specifically National Goal 8, calls for parent participation in the social, emotional and academic growth of the child.

What is apparent in all these citations is that the following kinds of involvement seem to be important in any school-based program: Parental ownership in the curriculum process, shared responsibility in the education of the child, constant communication, incorporation of parents in decision-making process in the school, emphasis on responsible parenting, availability of resources, and any and all elements that contribute to making the parent / family feel welcome in the school.

Sumter School District 17's parent involvement program is a Parent Education model that includes the following components: computer skills classes for parents, a parent resource mobile unit, school and district-sponsored workshops, monthly newsletters, a parent resource center, parenting skills home visitation services, and parent centers in each elementary school. The mission of the parenting program is to support the goals of and assist parents in the pursuit of happy, well-rounded, and educated children to meet the demanding challenges of the global society. Based on the Six National Standards of Parental Involvement (Volunteering, Parenting, Communicating, Learning At Home, Decision-Making and Collaboration with Community), the program consist of General Program Activities of workshops, national and state endorsed curriculums for parent education and collaborations with the county, adult education, district-level human resources and higher education institutions in the area.

The first major objective of the program is to foster parenting skills, job skills, and literacy skills through collaboration with agencies. This is done through a parenting skills home visitation programs with funding provided through the Governor's office, school and district parenting workshops, and computer skills / education provided through the county's adult education program. From assistance to parents of children from pre-natal to age five through the home visitation program to parenting-skills workshops and computer literacy classes, the program has supported the needs of its parents. Another collaboration between the county's Adult Education program provided computer literacy to reduce the technology gap for parents. For example, after attending a computer literacy class, one course participant said, "My grandchildren were a step ahead of me. Now when they ask me a question, I'll be able to answer it." The school district has developed multiple ways for parents to have access to resources. Parents may check out materials such as educational toys, cassette tapes, assistive devices, books, puzzles and games from the school parent center, the parent resource center or the parent resource mobile. To foster volunteerism, all parent centers are staffed with volunteer parents who devote countless hours to working with parents who come to the centers for assistance and to manage the day-to-day operations of the centers. School and district workshops are offered throughout the year on a variety of subjects including test-readiness for the state's assessment program (Palmetto Achievement Challenge Test), positive discipline, and grade level academic skills. Additionally, computer skills classes for parents are held at each elementary school.

The second major program objective is to increase parental awareness of ways that they can become involved in their children's school The principal and staff of each school, as well as the district office, are committed to creating an atmosphere that is favorable to parental involvement and are supportive of parent participation in the education of children. School District 17 developed its program with the idea of being parent-friendly. In order to do this, the school district formed a collaboration with the CHEC / LEA Teacher

Quality Enhancement Partnership. This collaboration allowed the school to take an aggressive approach to communicating with parents through business-type advertising strategies: mission statements, flyers, paraphernalia with the parent involvement logo, newspaper articles regarding services, special events at the parent centers, information on the district's website, parent newsletters, articles in the district's state-mandated annual "Report to the Community" and visits to public housing sites. Using a business approach to build parents' awareness of the school's desire to have them take active roles in the school has been an integral part of the school district's parental involvement efforts. Parents serve on improvement councils, participate in the writing of school renewal plans and become a part of the educational program through parent / school compacts. The outcomes are 1) parental partnership in the decision-making process of the schools, 2) increased parent volunteerism, attendance at parent-teacher conferences, participation at school-sponsored events, utilization of the resources in the parent centers and 3) increased student performance on the state mandated assessment (Palmetto Achievement Challenge Test).

Parent involvement ought not be incorporated into schools just because of legislation, national movements and national centers of research. Educators must lay the foundations by developing programs and conveying expectations in school settings that continue to aggressively promote the importance of parents in the education of their children.

References

Baker, A.J. & Soden, L. M. (1998). *The Challenges of Parent Involvement Research, ERIC Clearinghouse on Urban Education*, New York, NY.

Chavkin, N. F. & & Williams, D. L. (1988). *Critical Issues in Teacher Training for Parent Involvement. Educational Horizons*, Volume 66, Number 2.

Comer, J.P. (1988). Is Parenting Essential to Good Teaching? *NEA Today*, 6, 34-40.

Educators Notebook On Family Involvement: Programs, Plans and Ideas, (2000). Parent Institute: University of Oregon.

Epstein (1995). School / Family / Community Partnerships: Caring for the Children We Share, Phi Delta Kappan, 76 (9).

National Standards for Parent / Family Involvement Programs. (1998). National PTA: Chicago.

www.ncreal.org, 2002

www.nwrel.org, 2003

T-3 Teacher Certification Program – A National Model

Dr. Cash Kowalski, Professor
South Carolina State University

Dr. Nancy Cassidy Dunlap
Associate Director, School of Education
Clemson University
and
Dr. Kathy LaBoard Brown,
Assistant Professor, The Citadel

(L - R) Dr. Cash Kowalski, Dr. Nancy Dunlap, Dr. Kathy Brown

The South Carolina Transition-to-Teaching (T3) Coalition has designed a teacher certification program to provide requisite training and credentialing for retiring military personnel to become teachers in the schools most in need. Incorporating a unique blend of on-line instruction and hands-on practical experiences, the program is accessible around the clock and around the world. Participants may begin training within two years of retirement and, through a special Proviso by the state legislature, are classified as resident students at the four partner universities. The curriculum, grounded in a documentable knowledge base, reflects what a new, second-career professional needs to know and be able to do to become an effective teacher. Featuring a robust curriculum, a powerful e-learning delivery mode, a strong research and evaluation component, a year-long paid internship and follow-up with skilled mentor-teachers, this program has the capacity for ameliorating the teacher shortage in South Carolina and elsewhere. This unique program prepares a new generation of teachers for our schools–teachers with prior leadership experience and skills, a mature intellectual disposition, and a world view that will transfer well to the teaching profession.

The National Commission on Teaching and America's Future concluded that the reform of teacher education must start with the restructuring of its foundation – the teaching profession. Qualified teachers are the single most powerful variable in explaining the differences in student achievement; quality teachers are a more powerful factor in student learning than socioeconomic status (*What Matters Most: Teaching America's Future*, 1996).

No Child Left Behind Act of 2001, requires schools to have a "highly qualified" teacher placed in every classroom by 2005-2006. The law invokes a host of characteristics, including a teacher's academic preparation, especially advanced degrees, subject/content knowledge, classroom behavior, classroom management, and appropriate educational experience, among others

(Berliner, 2002). Dr. Gerardo Gonzalez, Dean, School of Education of Indiana University (2002) has stated that critical to learning is knowing how to teach. According to Gonzalez, teachers must have developed skills in teaching so that they are capable of motivating students to learn precisely what they need to know and be able to do. Teachers must have the knowledge and skills to develop challenging, interesting, and stimulating lessons.

The South Carolina T3 Coalition has developed a program using "blended learning" (e-learning and practical, hands-on field experiences) to enable the participants to actualize their potential as teachers while concurrently ameliorating the teacher-shortage needs in South Carolina. The Coalition is preparing candidates who (a) will work in small rural or inner-city schools, (b) will earn certification and "highly qualified" teaching status, and (c) will increase minority and male presence in the teaching force.

To be successful, aspiring teachers need more than a textbook and a handshake. They need training–not a traditional undergraduate teacher-training program (although these options continue to be available), but one tailored specifically for them, to provide necessary knowledge and skills, to provide options for demonstration of proficiency, to avail them of what they need to be successful in this social structure called "school," while acknowledging the talents, experience, and expertise that they bring with them.

The South Carolina T3 Coalition consists of four institutions, five agencies, and a corporate partner; Clemson University, the University of South Carolina, The Citadel, and South Carolina State University have come together with five agencies (the South Carolina Center for Educator Recruitment, Retention, and Advancement, the Employment Security Commission, the Commission on Higher Education, the State Department of Education, and the Governor's Office) and IBM/Lotus to craft an initiative to enable commissioned and non-commissioned officers with college degrees to secure the requisite training and credentialing to become teachers.

The targeted group consists of members of the armed forces, commissioned or non-commissioned officers, who possess a bachelor's degree or higher. The reasons to tap this talented pool are numerous:

1. The military began downsizing in 1994, sending well-qualified personnel into the civilian work force.
2. Military personnel often have strong content skills, particularly in math and science.
3. Commissioned and non-commissioned officers possess high levels of training and education; most have extensive military training experience.

4. The potential pool is great.
5. Within the ranks exists a high ethnic minority ratio.
6. Likewise, there is a high ratio of males; this cadre can provide more men for the classrooms.
7. Their military experience as trainers provides them with a solid foundation for a teaching career.
8. They have the added benefit of being trained in providing safe and secure environments.
9. In their military careers, they have gained organizational, interpersonal, technical, technology, and leadership skills.
10. They are great role models for kids; they are mature, physically fit, and drug-free.
11. Finally, they bring a wealth of personal and professional experiences and a world view to our classrooms.

Because of their high degree of training and education acquired during their military service, because the number of teachers who can be trained from this pool is potentially much greater than many sources, and because of the high ethnic minority and gender ratios which could significantly ameliorate under-representation of ethnic minorities and men in these critical-needs areas of education, this group would be a benefit to and a resource for South Carolina's schools and our young people.

Evolution of T3 ARC

The T3 ARC began in August 1999; the first year was dedicated to planning. With a small grant, the Coalition undertook a rigorous process to design an alternative certification program to allow participants to complete their requisite course work while still on active duty using e-learning and blended-learning strategies.

The coalition reviewed the existing literature on alternative certification, best practice, and research to examine the programs of other states, teacher education programs, and other entities. While most states have developed or are developing routes for alternative licensure, none possesses the uniqueness of the South Carolina model.

Based on the premise posited in What Matters Most, a report of the National Commission Teaching and America's Future, "What teachers know and can do is the most important influence on what students learn." The Coalition began by processing ten essential questions:

1. What do mature, new, second-career teachers need to know?
2. What do mature, new, second-career teachers need to be able to do?

3. What specific competencies do they need?
4. What specific competencies do they possess and can they demonstrate?
5. How do we identify these competencies?
6. How do we identify gaps?
7. Can we develop a training model based on this gap analysis?
8. What will it include?
9. How can we deliver it? Can we deliver it via the Internet?
10. What resources (human, material, technological) do we need for this?

Upon completion of this analysis, the Coalition then reviewed standards, best practice, knowledge bases, and research from the following agencies and organizations, among others:

- National Board for Professional Teaching Standards (NBPTS)
- National Association for Accreditation of Teacher Education (NCATE)
- American Association of Colleges of Teacher Education (AACTE)
- Interstate New Teacher Assessment and Support Consortium (INTASC)
- National Network for Educational Renewal (NNER)
- Good Teaching Matters: A Report of the Education Trust
- Institutional Conceptual Frameworks
- Carnegie Foundation for the Advancement of Teaching

The Coalition also adopted the following "touchstones" to guide the process and to keep the group on-track and on-target:

"Develop high-quality pathways to teaching for recent graduates, mid-career changers, paraprofessionals already in the classroom, and military and government retirees." National Commission on Teaching & America's Future, What Matters Most, (Recommendation 3).

"The fundamental differences between an alternative and traditional program are the target audience, the training design, and the length of training, not the program content, rigor, or expected outcomes." AACTE, Alternative Preparation for Licensure: Policy Statement.

"To do and perform all things necessary to encourage, uphold, and dignify the profession of teaching." Carnegie Foundation for the Advancement of Teaching and Learning.

The Coalition would return to these touchstones often.

The Curriculum

Upon examination of the standards of evidence, the Coalition developed two documents: (1) What teaches need to know and (2) what teachers need to be able to do. To achieve the necessary validation, these lists were widely circulated within and without South Carolina; teachers, teacher educators, parents, business people, community leaders, and the Military Assistance Council, the advisory group for the Coalition, had the opportunity for input. It was important that this review be as comprehensive, as valid, and as reliable as possible.

The result is a rich, valid, robust curriculum, grounded in best practice and research, based upon what career-changing professionals need to know and be able to do to become successful teachers, (acknowledging that pedagogy for a 40-year-old professional should differ from that for a 20-year-old college sophomore AND recognizing the vast expertise and experience that military professionals bring to the profession) in nine discrete modules divided into three blocks, from the more general and theoretical to the more specific and concrete:

Block One
- Psychological Foundations of Adolescent Learning and Development
- Technology in the Classroom
- Cultural Distinctions and Diversity

Block Two
- Community Resources
- Application of Research
- Student Assessment and Evaluation

Block Three
- Methods and Strategies (content-specific in mathematics, sciences, and English/language arts)
- Classroom Organization and Management
- The Culture that is School

The Technology

The group then, upon returning to the "Ten Essential Questions," determined that it could, indeed, take this list of what teachers need to know and, using a "gap analysis," could tailor an individualized, performance-based, upon-entry program based upon the client's documented experiences and expertise, over the World-wide Web, using state-of-the-art technology and synchronous and asynchronous delivery of modules rather than traditional graduate-level courses.

From this point, the Coalition turned to the technology experts; upon reflection, it was determined that the program required a vehicle not only of getting the courses on-line, but also a means of managing variable credit, matriculation processes and systems, generating student transcripts, providing means of interactivity between faculty and participants, among other significant issues, and an in-depth review of technological potential yielded two likely candidates; IBM/Lotus remains as a partner in crafting the technological methodology for on-line delivery and management of this complex project. The support and engagement of IBM/Lotus has been exemplary; not only is their LearningSpace a robust system, but their technical support has been exceptional.

The Academic Program

Military personnel may access the program during their last two years of active duty through the T3 Coalition Teacher Certification Program Website (http://www.hehd.clemson.edu/TTT/). Since all of these persons will have bachelor's degrees (and many will come with master's degrees), content expertise is presumed; however, prior to admission into the program, the candidate must provide passing scores from the Praxis II subject-area examination to validate currency of content knowledge. The candidate's program is determined based upon what experiences he/she can validate from the military. University faculty provides the personalization.

The participant has the modules available around the clock, and the professors maintain maximum availability. Options are available, also, for real-time discussions, chat rooms, white boards, and the like. Additionally, since teacher education cannot occur in a vacuum, field experiences and practical applications of skills are built into each module. Upon completion of the modules, the participant is placed in a one-year internship in a high-need school.

Project Uniqueness

The project is unique in many ways:

- Participants may begin within two years of separation from military service.
- Participants may participate at their duty station, anywhere in the world.
- Program uses state-of-the-art technology.
- Participants are provided a waiver of out-of-state tuition.
- Participants partake of a robust curriculum designed to prepare them for the realities of the classroom.
- Coordination among 4 universities and 5 agencies, school districts, and a corporate partner; over 90 people have been involved in the genesis of this project.

- Field experiences and practical application of skills are incorporated into every course.
- Curriculum developed by university faculty based on what teachers need to know and be able to do.
- Graduate-credit modules via Internet delivery with synchronous and asynchronous options.
- One-year paid internship with skilled mentor teacher; participants will not miss a paycheck.
- Placement in districts with greatest need.
- Strong research/evaluation component.
- Focus on retiring military with bachelor's degree or higher.
- Program availability year-round with course rotation.
- Flexibility.
- Plans are in development for national rollout.

The result is a program that is research-based, facile to use and to navigate, easy to access, is valid, is reliable, and is grounded in reality and a scientifically documentable knowledge base.

The result will be a new category of teacher–a teacher with important and transferable experiences, leadership, and skills–who has demonstrated a maturity, a world view, an "intellectual disposition," and a grounding in his or her subject matter.

This new generation of professional career-changers who become teachers should provide to American classrooms a role model who can deliver the kind of quality education envisioned in the *No Child Left Behind Act of 2001.* Military personnel and veterans represent a wealth of talent, experience, diversity, knowledge, expertise, skills, and world views. What opportunities exist to install this leadership and talent in the inner city and rural schools most in need!

References

Bracey, G.W. (2002). The 12th Bracey report on the condition of public education. *Phi Delta Kappan* 84 (2), 135-149

Darling-Hammond, Chung, R. and Frelow, F. (2002). Variation in teacher preparation: How well do different pathways prepare teachers to teach? *Journal of Teacher Education*, 53 (4), 286-303

Darling-Hammond, L. (1996). What matters most: a competent teacher for every child. *Phi Delta Kappan*, V. 78, No. 3, 193-98.

Gonzalez, G. (2001). Knowing how to teach is critical to learning. NCATE: The Standard of Excellence in Teacher Preparation (news briefs). http://www.ncae.org/.

Kerr, I.L. & Berliner, D.C. (2002). The Effectiveness of "teach for America" and Other Under-certified Teachers on Student Academic Achievement: A Case of Harmful Public Policy, *Education Policy Analysis Archives*, V. 10, No. 37.

Schroeder, C. C. (1998). Collaboration and Partnerships. ACPA - Higher Education Trends for the Next Century.

No Child Left Behind Act of 2001, Pub. L. No. 107-110 , Stat. 1425, (2002).

What Matters Most: Teaching for America's Future (online) (Sept. 1996). http://www.nctaf.org/publications/what matters most.pdf

Beyond the Basics: Encouraging Classroom Inquiry in High Needs Schools

Dr. Jane F. Zenger, Professor
University of South Carolina

Unexpected changes are occurring in high needs schools where creative, innovative teachers have taken on expanded leadership roles. This article chronicles cultural and curriculum changes taking place in seven University of South Carolina Professional Development Schools where coaching teachers and interns conduct classroom research, co-teach university courses and infuse inquiry into a test-driven curriculum. A DOE Title II funded Teacher Quality Partners Project provides University clinical support to implement, evaluate, and disseminate the model projects.

Inquiry-based teaching has become the intense focus in seven Columbia, South Carolina Professional Development schools where preservice teachers are placed to complete student teaching internships. Coaching teachers in these schools are working in tandem with University of South Carolina faculty to enhance student achievement and encourage inquiry-based instruction. A DOE funded Title II Teacher Quality Project (the TQC) in the USC College of Education supports and oversees this work, annually funding classroom inquiry mini-grants in pre-k-12 schools. The TQC has focused on developing "Teachers as Leaders" and on strengthening school/university collaboration. The schools participating in the five-year initiative are: Bradley Elementary School, Horrell Hill Elementary School, Hyatt Park Elementary School, Meadowfield Elementary School, Summit Parkway Middle School, Crayton Middle School and Dreher High School. All of these schools are part of a Professional Development School (PDS) network. USC preservice teachers are placed with coaching teachers in PDS schools to complete both practicum and student teaching internships. For that reason, it is important that the coaching/mentor teachers in these schools model the very best practices possible. Action research and inquiry-based teaching are two methods that are emphasized in university classes and supported in the project schools.

To advance these strategies, the coaching teachers in the partner schools are invited to submit mini-grant proposals for action research related to inquiry based curriculum reform. The mini-grant projects that have been developed in the past several years are transforming these schools and having an impact on how teachers teach and how students learn.

Teachers and students who participate in inquiry-based classrooms conduct self-directed studies and examine issues from multiple points of view. They are encouraged to work cooperatively and submit project reports, personal reflections and student documentation. Some projects are teacher directed and other projects are student directed. John Barell explains this duel concept in his book, Developing More Curious Minds. He explains that, " This spectrum suggests that there are times when we need to make the most of the decisions regarding curricular questions to be answered; times when we negotiate these with our students: and other times when we follow the lead of students' interests and concerns, allowing them to make most of the decisions." (p.32)

One of the first steps in implementing inquiry is to define the type of inquiry and persuade teachers that this type of instruction is effective. Teachers are often hesitant to veer away from the type of traditional teaching that they have always used. The role of the university faculty is to support the transition from traditional teaching at every step of the way. The university liaisons assist teachers as they develop lesson plans and locate additional resources. There is flexibility in what can be funded but it usually involves additional classroom resources, teacher designed graduate courses and/or content specialists who might evaluate science or math programs.

Since it is a non-exact science, teachers often need to be reminded that inquiry is a process that requires patience, flexibility, creativity and reflection. For those unfamiliar with the inquiry process, divergent discussions and individual research in the classroom can be viewed as a chaotic process. However, the USC study is finding that once teachers and students experience inquiry at its best, it is hard to go back to a traditional format. The power of student debate and individualized study reflects an energized democratic process where many ideas and viewpoints are represented. In a time when teachers are often conflicted about the amount of time they must spend "teaching to the test" and standardizing instruction for diverse children, the idea of using inquiry to motivate underachieving students and inspire critical thinking is being embraced by teachers as a way to bring the creative spark back into the classroom.

According to Maxine Greene (1995) by, "Refusing externally provided multiple-choice tests and being willing to see things big when they encounter students, teachers can devise the modes of teaching that are appropriate for these persons, that can launch them in diverse ways into what we now understand as inquiry (p.13).

The teachers participating in inquiry-based teaching report that the students have more opportunities to integrate information and think critically. Teachers report that the answer to one inquiry question often leads to other questions and applications. Thus, inquiry-based teaching opens the door for expanded student discussion and introspection. The world seems more accessible to students who have had the opportunity to learn via authentic problem solving and real world research. Teachers become facilitators and questions often take on a new meaning. Questions are not just used to test facts, but also to push students to the next level of critical thinking.

In just four years, the support of inquiry research in the targeted schools has increased from nine reported projects to over seventy activities and units related to inquiry. Many of the units and long-term lessons have been incorporated into a school-wide curriculum. For example, at Horrell Hill Elementary School, an ecology unit to study recycling and the environment has become an annual school program. For the past two years the students have been recognized by WIS TV and DEHEC as "Champions of the Environment."

Hyatt Park Elementary has established an afternoon program that brings in African-American male role models as "Real Men" to read to and mentor children with behavior problems. The program is having a positive effect on the children's classroom behavior and their interest in reading and homework. More significantly, the teachers and students are discovering that the process of inquiry based teaching often leads to unexpected results.

Preliminary results of reading and math test scores show an upward trend in the schools where inquiry is being implemented. Six of the teachers that have participated in the inquiry projects have been selected teacher of the year in their school or district. Nancy James' fifth grade students at Hyatt Park Elementary won the 2002 top honor in the Richland District One Visual Literacy Bookmaking award. The interdisciplinary project combined computer graphics, creative writing and historical content based on studies of ancient Egypt.

Project Design

The inquiry projects are developed and supported through a school leadership or "Context" team. Twice a month a small team of 3-5 classroom teachers meets with the University liaisons to develop ideas to extend the use of inquiry strategies. Teachers decide how they might enhance a unit or lesson using inquiry in either an individual classroom, in the grade level or as a school wide project. If additional resources or outside consultants are needed, the teachers submit a mini-grant for funding books, materials or software.

These mini-grants traditionally fall into three categories: basic inquiry, inquiry based on a service-learning project, and/or support of preexisting programs such as the South Carolina Reading Initiative. Funding per project ranges from $250.00 to $2,000 depending on the scope and number of students impacted.

The collaboration effort reflected in this work is part of the PDS philosophy at USC that teachers should be supported in their efforts to investigate educational strategies that meet the needs of children in their school. Teaching through inquiry requires the teacher to be reflective and responsive. The teacher becomes a "lifelong learner"- constantly expanding and updating his/her content knowledge base. Inquiry into a subject might last from one or two weeks or students might accumulate data throughout the schools year.

Often, the projects involve parents and/or the community. For example, one class explored the link between computer assisted math tutorials and regular math remediation. Presphonia Perkins at Hyatt Park used computers, trade books and the Public Television Reading Rainbow series to help emergent readers develop visual schema about the world.

At Horrell Hill Elementary, parents unfamiliar with computers worked alongside their children creating family web sites. Children at Bradley Elementary conducted a service-learning program focused on fire safety and the plight of the homeless. Almost all projects were interdisciplinary in nature and in one school, fifth graders in a science club combined art and science in a project to dissect and create anatomical drawings of squids and worms.

In each of these projects, the university liaison and classroom teachers first defined the academic environment of the school and the children. The research agenda represented the culture and needs of the particular school as opposed to having a university imposed research agenda. In this way, teachers developed authentic studies connected to state standards and directed at the area/s apt to have the most impact on student achievement.

Using inquiry and designing classroom research requires teachers to reflect on their own abilities and talents. The process of inquiry begins with a series of teacher directed questions. What will make you a better teacher? What are your talents and the talents of your students? What are your instructional strengths and weaknesses? What are you doing to assure a democratic classroom? What are your students' greatest needs? What talents, gifts and learning styles can you enhance? What are your community resources? How much additional funding will you need to carry out this innovation?

With their students' needs in mind, teachers are encouraged to refine lesson plans and teaching strategies. The university faculty is available to help teachers define and conceptualize a successful outcome and determine what type of assessment and/or documentation might best show evidence of student learning.

In the first two years of the project, teachers were skeptical. They worried that inquiry based teaching might not guarantee the same results as traditional practices. This hesitation about using inquiry is a natural reaction to non-traditional teaching. It is described in Learning through Inquiry: From Columbus to Integrated Curriculum (Short, Schroeder, Laird, Kauffman, Ferguson, & Crawford, 1996). Their study describes the philosophical transformation when teachers began seeing teaching as more than a mastery of, "specific facts, procedures and skills"(p.10). Inquiry isn't just asking and answering questions. In fact, "learners will not pursue the questions that really matter in their lives unless they are in an environment where their ideas and lives are valued" (p.11). Many educators of today see inquiry in the classroom as crucial in the maintenance of a democratic society.

Ducharme and Ducharme (1999) discuss the importance of inspiring students to want to learn and the best teachers will, "guide them into becoming independent learners, assist them in exploring complicated issues, and facilitate students' growth in personal autonomy" (p.359). Inquiry and developing a classroom of choice may become a student's entry into " under-standing the world" and "becoming participatory citizens" (p.359). Success often comes through learning a process and the result may be teaching students a strategy for learning rather than a narrow set of skills or facts. In this manner, learning is tied to exploration and the excitement of discovery motivates both the teacher and learner.

Teachers using inquiry in the project schools have reported that the students retained more information because they were not only required to recite facts and information, but also had to demonstrate the ability to apply and synthesize that knowledge. Kay Ratliff, a third grade teacher at Meadowfield Elementary commented that because of inquiry, "The children are more deeply connected to issues and ideas". Over 95% of the teachers who developed and implemented inquiry units reported that inquiry was in their curriculum to stay.

Saudah Collins, a second grade teacher in a small rural school was so afraid of animals that she felt her efficiency as a science teacher was impaired. Her discomfort, especially around reptiles and insects, was a personal obstacle preventing her personal and professional development. Saudah was determined to overcome these issues and her inquiry project began as a "teacher's journey to feel more at ease with creatures in the natural world" and has evolved into an environmental nature lab filled with snakes, geckos, insects, and newts. Crickets are raised for the reptiles, a classroom garden is maintained, and organic materials are composted. There is a virtual zoo in her room and a small reptile/fish pond in the walled garden just outside her classroom. This learning environment has created a sense of familiarity and confidence with the natural world. Today, Saudah's successful project has expanded into a service-learning project with her students visiting other schools and teaching other children what they have learned about ecology and the environment. Her students have twice been featured by DEHEC and featured on WIS TV commercials as "Champions of the Environment".

An excellent example of a single-class long-term project takes place every year at Summit Middle School. David Chadwell, a sixth grade Social Studies teacher at Summit Parkway Middle School, has developed a side-by-side curriculum in which students define civilization and create their own country. In his semester long inquiry project, students create a government, a form of currency, and resources related to their country's geology and geography. They create trade routes, define geographical and climatic conditions and by the end of the semester, "trade days" are instituted and the community is invited to participate.

David has discovered that student research and writing is often more accurate and advanced when students learn though inquiry. His research on student achievement is showing interesting trends for motivating underachievers in both reading and writing. Students who are building their own civilization show a deeper understanding and interest in history when they study maps and read textbooks. They ask more questions and do extended web-based research. Teams of students conduct in-depth studies about ancient art, government, and economics along with other aspects of civilization that they need to develop their own culture.

Teachers, interns and university faculty have learned that inquiry is not a process that can be mandated or incorporated into a curriculum with one lesson plan or unit of study. It will not transform a classroom or school in a day or even a year. The process of inquiry is effective only when it becomes a way of thinking about learning. Teachers in the project reported that inquiry instruction is beginning to permeate every aspect of their teaching and planning. They agree that inquiry takes practice and patience; however, teaching through inquiry is definitely worth the effort because inquiry provides opportunities for students to experience the gratification of learning how to learn.

Both teachers and students appreciate the opportunities for teamwork and cooperative learning activities.

The power of inquiry-based teaching is that it yields authentic assessment, and that may prove to be an important balance in a standards driven school and society. There is no doubt that our children face a complex and information dominated world. As teachers and teacher educators we must do all we can to prepare our children to seek the truth and maintain integrity. "Teachers must be sources of vision for as many learners as they can. They must be sources of relief from the external world: their classrooms must be safe and sane places for human relationships to evolve"(Ducharme & Ducharme, 1999, p.361). At its best, inquiry moves beyond the basics, revealing the importance of student ideas, the diversity of approach in problem solving, and most importantly, the power of learning as a lifelong, self-directed endeavor.

To learn more about the schools and teachers participating in the Teacher Quality Collaborative visit "inquiry" link at http://tqc.ed.sc.edu or contact Dr. Jane Zenger in the College of Education, University of South Carolina, Columbia, SC , 29208 (zengerj@gwm.sc.edu).

References

Barell, J. (2003). *Developing More Curious Minds.* Alexandria, VA. Association for Supervision and Curriculum Development.

Ducharme, E.R. & Ducharme, M.K. (1999). Responding to Goodlad: The Primacy of Teacher Education in SCDE's. , *Journal of Teacher Education, Vol.50, 5, 358-362.*

Greene, M. (1995). *Releasing the Imagination: Essays on Education, the Arts, and Social Change.* San Francisco, CA: Jossey-Bass Inc.

Myers, C., & Simpson, D. (1998). *Re-Creating Schools: Places Where Everyone Learns and Likes It.* Thousand Oaks, CA: Corwin Press, Inc.

Sirotnik, K. (1990). *Society, Schooling, Teaching and Preparing to Teach.* In J. Goodlad, R. Soder, & K. Sirotnik (Eds.), The Moral Dimensions of Teaching. (pp.296-327). San Francisco, CA: Jossey-Bass Inc.

Short, K., Schroeder, J., Laird, J., Kauffman, G., Ferguson, M., & Crawford K.M. (1996). *Learning Through Inquiry: From Columbus to Integrated Curriculum*, York, Maine, Stenhouse Publishers.

Cross Registration – Articulation Pathways to Success

By
Dr. Howard D. Hill
Vice President for Academic Affairs
Claflin University

(L-R) Dr. James Arrington, V.P. Academic Affairs, SCSU; Dr. Howard D. Hill, Dr. Walter A. Tobin, Jr., V.P. Academic Affairs, Orangeburg-Calhoun Technical College

The Community Higher Education Council (CHEC), established April 25, 1997, forged a Cross-Registration Agreement and an Admissions Agreement Alliance for the mutual benefit of Claflin University, Orangeburg-Calhoun Technical College and South Carolina State University. These agreements were designed to (1) enhance higher education opportunities in the community, and (2) to provide students greater access to shared facilities, instructional services (including distance education capabilities), etc., and in most cases, without direct cost to them. CHEC is a viable education partnership that is working well by fostering non-competing higher education goals in close collaboration.

The Community Higher Education Council (CHEC) was formally established in Orangeburg, South Carolina, April 25, 1997. The presidents of Claflin University, Dr. Henry N. Tisdale; Orangeburg-Calhoun Technical College, Dr. Jeffrey Olsen; and South Carolina State University, Dr. Leroy Davis, forged an alliance to form a Cross-Registration Agreement and an Admissions Agreement for the mutual benefit of each institution. In this regard, these agreements were designed to (1) enhance higher education opportunities in the community, and (2) to provide students greater access to shared facilities, greater instructional services (including distance education capabilities), etc., and in most cases, without a direct cost to them.

As a result of these two agreements, CHEC is a viable education partnership that is working well by fostering non-competing goals in close collaboration. Through these agreements, CHEC also is tying together the resources of the partner institutions by meeting the individual and collective needs of students, the home and host institutions where the students are enrolled, and others desirous of participating in unique educational experiences. Cross Registration in the CHEC education community in Orangeburg is a plan designed for emulation and adoption by other education entities.

In significant ways, the current CHEC presidents (Dr. Ann Crook, president of Orangeburg-Calhoun Technical College and Interim President Ernest Finney of South Carolina State University have replaced Dr. Olsen and Dr. Davis, respectively), have made a concerted commitment to develop stronger ties, linkages, and collaborative activities to usher in systematic change within and among member institutions. These are the revised guidelines that govern the Cross-Registration Agreement and the Admission Agreement:

Cross-Registration Policies (Revised and Approved in 2002)

1. Undergraduate students may participate in the Agreements:

- if they are in good standing at their home institution;
- if they have paid full-time tuition and fees at their home institution (and, therefore, will not have to pay tuition for an extra course taken at the host campus);
- if after declaring full-time status at their home institution, may register for not more than one (1) free course per semester per institution at the other participating CHEC member institutions;
- if the course at the host institution is not offered concurrently at the home institution (i.e., not offered at a reasonably scheduled time);
- if they meet the prerequisite requirements of the host institution; and
- if the acquired approvals are obtained.

2. Part-time students will pay regular per-credit tuition and fee charges directly to the institution at which the course is taken.

3. Courses are available under this program only on a space-available basis, and registration occurs at the time designated by the host campus.

4. Special fees, such as laboratory fees and book fees, must be paid to the host institution and are not covered under the cross-registration policy.

5. All courses taken at the host campus will be transcripted and sent to and recorded by the home institution. The grades will be included by the home institution in academic calculations, meaning the grades received in the courses are computed in semester and/or quarters grade point averages.

6. Any exception to these policies must be approved in writing by the Vice President for academic Affairs at both the home and the host institutions.

Note: Summer academic sessions shall not be counted as eligible semesters (or quarters) for cross-registration purposes. Involved students must be legal South Carolina residents, and out-of-state students desirous of participating in the Cross-Registration and Admission Agreements must pay the difference between the in-state and out-of-state fees charged at Orangeburg-Calhoun Technical College and South Carolina State University. Claflin University does not charge differentiating fees for out of state students and international students.

Institutional Accountability

As institutions of higher education face increasing costs, dwindling funding and heightened accountability demands, these Cross-Registration and Admissions partnership offer the opportunity for sharing resources. Such sharing contributes not only to internal effectiveness and efficiency, but also to the delight of students through their appreciation of what the three institutions by providing them: the opportunity to enroll in courses at other than their home institutions on a friendly-arrangement basis. Through these agreements, many more classroom options are available to students, thus keeping them on track to graduate without delay or having to attend other Universities for desired courses and/or academic experiences.

CHEC and Alliance 2020

The local Community Higher Education Council is working in conjunction with Alliance 2020, which was formed through a grant provided by the W.K. Kellogg Foundation, to join South Carolina's Technical College System, South Carolina State University and Clemson University in this unique collaboration. It was, and is, part of a national effort to rethink the missions of colleges and how they serve their broader communities. The collaboration, to this point, is meeting its defined mission and objectives.

Alliance 2020 – Vision Statement
"Bridging the State ... Connecting the People"

In the year 2020, all communities in South Carolina are linked by a network of bridges, firmly anchored on strong supports and arching over waters that might otherwise engulf them. Open access to these bridges ensure a solid linkage between the past and future, local communities and the global village, rich and poor, urban and rural, into one healthy community of individuals empowered to lead rewarding and productive lives. Leadership in the development of the bridge system was and is provided by the partner institutions of Alliance 2020 – Claflin University, Orangeburg-Calhoun Technical College and South Carolina State University – which will continue to develop new bridges across other gulfs that reach to yet more distant horizons.

These measurable goals are being accomplished through activities akin to the following:

- Collaboration and cooperation in academic areas and student services;
- A seamless pathway for articulation;
- Sharing of resources and institutional talents;
- Participating in community events;

The benefits to the greater Orangeburg community will include but not be limited to:

- Contributions as resources for economic development;
- Opportunities for sharing a wide-range of socially enriching activities; and
- Sharing of facilities for partners and the community

As ambitious as the Cross-Enrollment Agreement and the Admissions Agreement partnership among Claflin University, South Carolina State University, and Orangeburg-Calhoun Technical College may be, Alliance 2020 certainly has provided enhanced opportunities for linkages among these stellar institutions and the students they serve. But the primary beneficiaries are – and as it should be – the involved students ... for their betterment.

The Community Higher Education Council (CHEC) does not discriminate on the basis of race, color, religion, sex, age, national origin, political affiliation, disability veteran or martial status in the administration of its educational policies, admissions policies, services and programs.

Collaborating for Integrating Content and Pedagogy: Preparing Preservice Teachers for P-12 Student Success

(L-R) Dr. Linda McIntyre, Dr. Verlie Tisdale

Dr. Linda R. McIntyre
NCATE Coordinator/Assistant Professor
School of Education
South Carolina State University

Dr. Verlie Tisdale
Division Chair
Natural Sciences & Mathematics
Claflin University

Collaborating for Integrating Content and Pedagogy: Preparing Preservice Teachers for P-12 Student Success, offers a shared vision of university level collaboration and construction of knowledge concerning content and pedagogy to improve the changing dynamics of preservice teacher preparation. In this article the authors examine the beginning understandings needed for integrating content and pedagogy in the teaching and learning process. The article concludes with implications, future directions, and suggestions for continued collaboration and research in interdisciplinary teacher preparation. The authors provide anecdotes that explicate the benefits of bridging content and pedagogy for preservice teacher training and P-12 student learning. The emergent need for integrating effective content and pedagogy instruction in preparing preservice teachers begins with researching and documenting promising interdisciplinary practices and learning experiences for P-12 contexts.

> *Subject matter and pedagogy have been particularly and persistently divided in the conceptualization and curriculum of teacher education. This fragmentation has teachers on their own with the challenge of integrating subject matter knowledge and pedagogy in the contexts of their work. (Ball 2000, p. 241)*

The authors clearly understand Ball's interpretation of the dilemmas inherent in the subject matter/pedagogy divide. Consequently, they came together from respective universities with disparate backgrounds to discuss and document experiences related to preservice teacher preparation in content and pedagogy. One is strictly a science content specialists and the other a language arts pedagogy educator. Prior to writing they exchanged ideas about their training and experiential backgrounds to begin the dialogue on developing appropriate relationships and integrating content and pedagogy at the university level. Each brought a very different philosophical and conceptual base, divergent understandings, and approaches to the context. A vision emerged, specifically collaboration and construction of understandings to improve the changing dynamics of preservice teacher preparation. In this article we examine the beginning understandings relevant to the need for an integrated content and pedagogy teaching and learning process. In addition, the article offers conclusions and implications for continued collaboration and research in interdisciplinary teacher preparation through anecdotes that explicate the benefits of bridging content and pedagogy.

Contemplating the need for integrating effective content and pedagogy instruction in preparing preservice teachers begins with P-12 contexts. First, integrating content and pedagogy merges theory and practice. Second, effective pedagogy and content instructional practices are aligned with high standards. Third, making connections–beginning the process of restructuring, integrating, and diminishing barriers between content specialists and pedagogy instructors is important. Collaborating at the university level has proven instructive for closing the subject matter and pedagogy divide. The following discussion will illuminate this process.

Merging Effective Content and Pedagogy

Effective teaching begins with integrating content and pedagogy. Restructuring the learning contexts for preservice teachers will influence P-12 instruction. The challenge of integrating theory and practice in academe and subject matter and pedagogy in the context of preservice and inservice teachers' work is dependent on changing habits of mind (Ball, 2000 & Dewey, 1964, 1933). Dewey's perspective on good teaching emphasizes the integral relationship between methods and content preparation. According to Dewey (1964) habits of mind must be established including the way content interacts and links with intellectual activity in children from childhood to adolescence. Typically, teachers have been left to their own devices to meet the challenges of incorporating subject matter knowledge and pedagogical strategies into the curriculum for youths. Dewey (1933) quite cogently conceptualized the marriage between theory and practice as simply "good teaching."

Thus, a major challenge for the broader community (including at the university across disciplines and methods instruction) is properly preparing preservice teachers in the areas of content and pedagogical practice. The challenge is evident because formal interdisciplinary relationships are nonexistent or not fully conceptualized, developed, or implemented. When preservice teachers learn to link content and pedagogy they evolve as new teachers who possess the knowledge, skills, and dispositions that adequately prepare them to serve P-12 students. Naturally, it follows that developing a strong foundation of teacher skills and knowledge is largely dependent on instituting a reform process changing from disparate content and pedagogy preparation to interdisciplinary holistic preparation (Darling-Hammond & Ball, 1996). What should emerge for preservice teachers is a program that promotes a depth of knowledge and capabilities across disciplines. Teachers must gain expertise in the content and proficiency in applying techniques related to methodology during instruction to overcome the complexities and difficulties of teaching and learning and to value high quality outcomes (Andrews, 1996).

Understanding subject matter in these ways provides a foundation for the pedagogical content knowledge that empowers teachers to represent ideas so that they are accessible to others. Knowledge of the domain of study is critical: the teacher needs to understand what ideas can provide important foundations for other ideas and understand what can be usefully linked and assembled (Darling-Hammond, 1997). Darling-Hammond's concept of linking and assembling preparation is useful in structuring preparation programs. There are two major forces that connect and guide South Carolina State University and Claflin University in their mission to bridge theory and practice for adequately preparing preservice teachers who influence P-12 student learning. First, the standards provide a framework for developing appropriate curriculum, praxis or heuristic practice for learners. University education and liberal arts programs should focus on aligning standards for effective content and pedagogy instruction. Second, structure is offered through a collaborative partnership grant enabling participants at all levels of educational development to embark upon reforming content and pedagogical instruction for all students.

Aligning High Standards for Effective Content and Pedagogy Instruction

"The teacher understands the central concepts, tools of inquiry, and structures of the discipline he or she teaches and can create learning experiences that make these aspects of subject matter meaningful for students." (INTASC Standard 1: Content and Pedagogy). Teacher preparation programs across the nation struggle to incorporate national, state, and local standards such as the previously stated standard. The National Council for Accreditation of Teacher Education (NCATE) standards and other standards emphasize developing appropriate abilities, dispositions, and knowledge in preservice and inservice teachers. They are required to learn central concepts, link prior knowledge to new learning experiences, employ appropriate resources and materials, integrate learning experiences across disciplines, and use effective methods of inquiry consistent with the standards.

Aligning instruction to the standards ensures that proper attention is given to fostering and nurturing content specialists and teacher educators' responsibilities in teacher preparation. Because standards-based instruction has been proven effective it naturally follows that content and pedagogy are interrelated and should be integrated into university programs for adequately preparing preservice teachers (http://www.ed.gov/inits/teachers/eisenhwer).

Thus, there is a need for continually structuring and integrating content and pedagogy curriculum and instruction for effective teacher education and content area discipline preparation. Both authors agree that the roles of national, state, and local standards and the Community Higher Education Council (CHEC) have been critical in supporting and effectuating the integration process and envisioning the enhancement of content and pedagogy preparation in each of their programs.

CHEC: Making Connections–Integrating Content and Pedagogy

At South Carolina State University and Claflin University, much like other universities, the gap between pedagogy and content continues. South Carolina State University via Earline Simms (former Dean of Education and Associate Vice President for Academic Affairs) led the way in establishing an existing program which provides an initial framework for changing the relationship among stakeholders in content and pedagogy preservice teacher preparation. The Community Higher Education Council (CHEC) collaborative program is supported by a Partnership to Reform Teacher Education in South Carolina.

The program aligns with the accrediting agencies' standards specifically, the National Council for Accreditation of Teacher Education, The National Board of Professional Teaching Standards (NBPTS), the Interstate New Teacher Assessment and Support Consortium (INTASC), and specialized professional association standards. Each of these accrediting bodies and learned societies requires and supports enhanced integration of content and pedagogy and performance evidence emanating the collaboration.

The Community Higher Education Council (CHEC) is an exemplary collaborative effort among South Carolina State University, Claflin University, Orangeburg-Calhoun Technical College, and Local Education Agencies. This Teacher Quality Enhancement Partnership is designed to restructure the preservice teacher preparation program emphasizes the following: strong academic discipline (subject matter) preparation, preparedness to teach ethnically and culturally diverse and mentally and physically challenged students, and recruiting academically capable students in math and science and other areas of critical need.

Understanding and creatively transforming curriculum in the teacher education program to meet the needs of P-16 students represents a supportive context for transforming programs. Anecdotal experiences offer powerful insight into the transforming mindset of university administrators, faculty, and students. The following anecdotes describe the nature of the evolving relationships established among the University and LEA participants and the results of the interactions and revelations found in the school context.

The first anecdote demonstrates the challenges faced by the mathematics and science content specialists and the teacher education professionals in an effort to diminish the content/pedagogy divide in the teacher education curriculum. The argument for integrating content and pedagogy is evident. This vignette materialized within the Division of Natural Sciences and Mathematics. When the Division Chair was first approached with the idea of partnering with Local Education Agencies (LEA) it was met with reluctance and skepticism. Reluctance stemmed from the fact that a group of professional scientist and mathematicians, and content area specialists, had little or no understanding of teacher education. Several were foreign born and had few experiences with the American secondary public school system. Others were educated in the public school system but had few experiences with mathematics and science. Although the university is small, faculty in the Divisions of Natural Sciences and Mathematics and Education were not well acquainted with each other. The greatest extent of their interactions came from seeing each other once a month at faculty meetings. Skepticism was rooted in philosophical differences, the level of incoming university students' facility of mathematics and science, and incongruent knowledge and methods base i.e., the style of teacher between the two divisions was divergent.

The need for transforming curriculum and improving relationships became very clear. The traditional thinking regarded by teacher educators as effective was not consistent with content specialists' perceptions. Nonetheless, the differences between Divisions, the preparedness of students for college mathematics and science, and the Divisions' high expectations for a competency-based mathematics and science curriculum offered an ideal opportunity to communicate and collaborate. CHEC was instrumental in the process for improving learning through integrating content and pedagogy. Division of Education and LEAs through the CHEC program focused on establishing appropriately reasonable expectations of incoming freshmen interested in pursuing science or mathematics teacher education or content specialty education.

The Division of Natural Sciences and Mathematics Chair decided to accompany tutors (college students) to one of the LEA sites. On the first visit, a tutor discovered that the middle school students were using inappropriate techniques to complete fractions. The tutor shared with other students the fact that some of the middle school students could not solve problems of fractions because they were not applying appropriate techniques. She asked middle school students to demonstrate step-by-step how they arrived at their answers. To the tutors' surprise, the middle school students all employed the same inappropriate process for solving the problems. Being careful not to bias students' perceptions of the problem, the tutors told the students they were going to teach them the "college way" to solve fractions. This tactic worked very well. The students learned how to work the problems without ever knowing they were using the wrong approach. The concept of completing the problems the "college way" instilled self-pride in the middle school students.

Throughout the semester, the tutors encountered similar problems. On each occasion, they were as diplomatic as they had been with the fractions. Ball states "understanding subject matter is essential to listening flexibly to others and hearing what they are saying or where they might be heading." This vignette shows that "knowing content is also crucial to being inventive in creating worthwhile opportunities for learning that take learner's experiences, interests, and needs into account" (Ball, 2000, p. 243).

Subsequently, the Natural Sciences and Mathematics Division Chair discovered that the teacher who taught those middle school students mathematics, as well as several others at the school were teaching out of field, therefore they were teaching science and mathematics courses for which they had no formal training. This incident gave the Natural Sciences and Mathematics Division Chair a better understanding of how some of the deficiencies witnessed at the college entry level may have developed. It also showed that there is indeed a need to recruit bright minds into the teaching profession and that the shortage of teacher education science and mathematics faculty at the secondary level affected student success at the college level.

The collaboration between Claflin University's Divisions of Natural Sciences and Mathematics and Education proved beneficial to the mathematics and science content area specialists because they came to understand what was meant by standards-based education. More importantly, they came to understand the importance of collaborating with educators and how to integrate the standards into their lectures while preparing students with strong academic backgrounds for a variety of careers, including teaching.

The second vignette relates the experiences of South Carolina State University participants. Similar to the Claflin University experience, the connection among SCSU School of Education faculty and content faculty is evolving. For example, in addition to faculty meetings, SCSU program coordinators, administrators and faculty representatives are members of the Teacher Education Council that convenes interdisciplinary faculty several times per year. SCSU is at the forefront in establishing a collaborative effort through CHEC and Professional Development Schools.

The School of Education's formal alliances across disciplines and at the P-12 school level are systematically organized with well-articulated goals and purposes. Relationships traverse the public schools and the university's laboratory school plus content specialists with the Schools of Engineering, Sciences, and Mathematics, Arts and Humanities, and Consumer Sciences. These formal linkages among the School of Education, other Schools, and P-12 schools can be attributed to the reform process instituted by the CHEC program and the accrediting agency, NCATE and the professional organizations in the respective fields. This is evidenced in the alignment of national, state, and local standards. These relationships have formed the foundation for strengthening teacher preparation in content and pedagogy. At the university level, some content area faculty and teacher education faculty have incorporated professional standards in the curriculum and course syllabi. In addition, pre-clinical and clinical experiences are driven by the interdisciplinary standards and form a basis for assessing candidates' performance. Interdisciplinary faculty members are university advisors who supervise candidates.

It is obvious that some of the traditional barriers dividing content and methods at SCSU are continually diminishing and making way for productive and positive interdisciplinary interactions while others remain intact. On one hand, the science educator in the Department of Teacher Education exerted tremendous effort to bring faculty together to bridge the content and methods programs in science. For example, a grant supporting a collaborative effort among science content and the science education components and NASA targets middle school students. These students will have planned opportunities for discovery learning experiences and simultaneously learning and applying science content in the contexts of the classroom and the NASA program. Nevertheless, some barriers remain which are being addressed through the accreditation process. Critical to resolving territorial issues is the commitment to infusing standards-based instruction, aligning standards and courses, and communicating these efforts honestly and openly.

Another less structured alliance was formed between SCSU's laboratory school and a Department of Teacher Education faculty member. The collaboration is between a middle grades science teacher and a language arts professor. This informal collaboration included meeting to discuss the needs of middle level students who are experiencing reading difficulty, particularly during content science instruction. The action plan created an opportunity for preservice teachers to apply the language arts techniques and strategies learned in the university classroom setting while simultaneously connecting pedagogy to content in school-based instruction. The faculty member and the science teacher possessed progressive stances on student preparation enabling them to cross boundaries and assimilate their efforts for the benefit of preservice teachers and middle school students. Similar alliances are occurring at all levels of schooling at South Carolina State University. Yet, such efforts need to be more systematic in order to solidify and advance the beginning initiatives of these and other stakeholders in education and content areas. Several lessons were learned through the collaboration between SCSU and Claflin University, as follows:

- University students and faculty are becoming more proficient in bridging content and pedagogy;
- P-12 students need more than content to succeed in the learning environment. It is imperative that pedagogy and content focus on the process and product of teaching and learning for P-12 students;
- Active and supportive collaborative relationships between content and pedagogy professionals interwoven into a systematic interdisciplinary teacher preparation program provides a first step towards changing perspectives on teaching and learning in P-12 schools; and
- Standards-based instruction is integral to the process. The article clearly illuminates the necessity to forge relationships between content area discipline specialists and teacher educators to transform standards-based instruction into the curriculum of the broader teaching and learning community.

Adequately serving diverse populations is critical to improving teacher competence and their knowledge, capabilities, and dispositions in developing and implementing quality culturally responsive curricula and instructional methods to meet all students' learning needs (Hollins & Oliver, 1999, Ball, 2000). This suggests it is important to design instruction that accounts for diverse students' background experiences and teachers' content preparation and proficiencies. Also evident through the vignettes is the issue of providing highly qualified teachers (content and pedagogical specialists) in effective education programs (Darling-Hammond, 1997).

Future Directions

There is a need to continue a critical review of the literature relevant to integrating content and pedagogy for preservice teacher education. Particularly to explicate the lessons provided by the Community Higher Education Council partnership—the literature supporting standards-based instruction, and the leadership of the University and LEA partnerships for transforming traditional divisions between content or discipline instruction, integrating methodological techniques into integrated interdisciplinary preparation for preservice teachers. University administrators, faculty, and students must continue conducting and analyzing research to support development of data emerging from the CHEC program and other initiatives at each of the partnership sites to influence what preservice teachers know and are able to do for P-12 students.

Suggested Activities

1. Specialized content area and teacher education faculty can plan together to create instructional activities and assessment instruments aligned with the standards.

2. Specialized content area and teacher education faculty can employ team-teaching techniques to encourage integration of content and pedagogy university and school-based instruction.

Structure programs for success through faculty seminars and training sessions to learn how to develop and implement techniques for high quality content and methods for addressing the curricular needs of diverse students.

Methods educators and content specialists should initiate collaborative groups to design a conceptual framework for education and content areas, integrating content pedagogy or content related methodological techniques.

Conclusion

In conclusion, the article has been instructive in relating the benefit of an organized and systematized effort to integrate content and pedagogy for preservice teacher preparation. The CHEC program provides an impetus for documenting future collaborations among participants at all levels of instruction, curriculum, and program development and implementation. Standards driven programs provide a framework for motivating and guiding content area specialists and teacher educators in the transformational process required of each school. Participants realize the significance of infusing standards-based content and pedagogy instruction at all levels of student development (P-16) and supporting P-12 students as they construct knowledge in the classroom.

References

Andrews, J., Garrison, D. R., & Magmusson, K. (1996). The teaching and learning transac tion in higher education: A study of excellent professors and their students. *Teaching in Higher Education*, 1, 81-103

Bransford, J. D., Brown, A. L., & Cocking, R. R. (Eds.). (1999). How people learn: Brain, mind, experience, and school. Washington, D.C.: National Academy Press.

Chatterji, M. (2002). Models and methods for examining standards-based reforms and accountability initiatives: Have the tools of inquiry answered pressing questions on improving schools? American Educational Research Association, 72 (3), 345-387.

Dewey, J. (1964). The relation of theory to practice in education. In R. D. Archambault (Ed.), John Dewey on education, (pp. 313-338). Chicago: University of Chicago Press.

Darling-Hammond, L. (1999). The right to learn: A blueprint for creating schools that work. San Francisco: Jossey-Bass.

Darling-Hammond, L. & Ball, D. (1996). Teaching for high standards: What policymakers need to know and be able to do. New York: Consortium for Policy Research in Education, with National Commission on Teaching and America's Future, for the National Goals Panel. (CPRE Joint Report Series).

Hollins, E. R. & Oliver, E. I. (Eds.) (2000).. Pathways to Success in School: Culturally Responsive Teaching. Mahwah, New Jersey: Lawrence Erlbaum Associates.

Simms, E., et al. (2000). Partnership to Reform Teacher Education in South Carolina: Community Higher Education Council. South Carolina State University.

The Report of the Carnegie Task Force on Learning in the Primary Grades. (1996). Years of Promise: A comprehensive learning strategy for America's children. Carnegie Corporation of New York.

Wang, J. & Odell, S. J., (2002). Mentored learning to teach according to standards-based reform: A critical review. American Educational Research Association. 72 (3) pp. 481-586.

Benefits of the Partnership

(Back L - R) Dr .Walter Tobin, Dr. Sandra Tonnsen; (front L-R) Dr. David Longshore, Mr. Melvin Smoak

Dr. David Longshore
Orangeburg Consolidated School District 4

Mr. Melvin Smoak
Orangeburg Consolidated School District 5

Dr. Walter Tobin
Calhoun County School District

Dr. Sandra Tonnsen
Orangeburg Consolidated School District 4

The partnership between Orangeburg Consolidated School Districts (OCSD) Three, Four and Five, the Calhoun County School District and the Community Higher Education Council (CHEC) has presented many positive opportunities for all involved. The partnership has created facilities-sharing opportunities for meetings and training plus professional development opportunities facilitated by faculty and staff from partnership institutions. Families in these communities have benefited from the partnership through parenting enhancement activities and health and wellness activities such as tennis lessons, swimming, nutrition workshops, health screenings, etc. As far as the public school districts are concerned, the opportunities for teacher preparation have been very important, given the push for education accountability and federal mandates like "No Child Left Behind." The largest school district — OCSD 5 took advantage of the partnership by establishing professional development schools to further enhance teacher training and improvement of instruction. However, the communities may be the big winners in this partnership because the combining of efforts to improve education by public schools, colleges and universities will inevitably, as has been the case here, produce positive results.

For Orangeburg Consolidated School Districts Three, Four and Five and the Calhoun County School District, the benefits of the partnership with the Community Higher Education Council (CHEC), which consists of Claflin University, Orangeburg Calhoun Technical College and South Carolina State University, have been many. For example, the partnership has done much for the Orangeburg and Calhoun County Communities because almost anytime educational entities in the same community can come together on one accord the results are going to be positive.

However, the benefits of the partnership reach much further than the one just mentioned. The partnership has created the opportunity for the sharing of facilities for meetings and training, as well as professional development opportunities that can be facilitated by faculty and staff members from the three institutions of higher education.

Parenting enhancement activities have also been a major benefit of the partnership between the four school districts, as well as, CHEC. These activities include parenting workshops and a Saturday Parent's Day, which consists of workshops featuring a nationally recognized speaker. Additionally, families have been provided information on and opportunities to participate in activities that promote wellness (tennis lessons, swimming, nutrition information, etc.).

From the perspective of the officials of the four school districts, one of the most important, as well as integral parts of the districts has been the area of teacher preparation. For example, 100 percent of the teachers hired by the districts from SCSU have earned a Bachelor's Degree and have met all state-mandated certification requirements. In this era of Education Accountability and "No Child Left Behind" legislation, it is of extreme importance for school districts to hire "highly-qualified" teachers, which by state and federal standards means, at the minimum, teachers who have met state certification requirements.

In Orangeburg Consolidated School District 5, the partnership has also led to the establishment of Professional Development Schools (PDS) at Whittaker Elementary School and William J. Clark Middle School. The Professional Development Schools have allowed the districts to initiate innovative strategies to provide highly capable teachers whose instruction will enhance the learning process.

The partnership has also provided assistance to a number of teachers who wanted to earn their M.Ed. degrees. It has assisted and continues to assist those teachers who are pursuing National Board Certification, a very involved and difficult process; however, the assistance of the partnership has been invaluable to many teachers undertaking this task.

Some of the other benefits of the partnership include the development of the skills pre-service teachers and university faculty need in using technology as a tool for improving their instruction and its delivery at all levels. The improvement of the leadership skills of teachers, principals, and superintendents through the establishment and implementation of the Institute for Effective Leadership will prove to be extremely beneficial.

All-in-all, the partnership between the Community on Higher Education Council, Orangeburg Consolidated School Districts Three, Four and Five, and the Calhoun County School District has been a "win-win" situation for all involved, and it has done much to enhance the relationship between these school districts and their higher education partners.

NetSchools Orion and Teacher Quality–Focus on Instructional Leadership, Standards and Professional Development

(L - R) Dr .Walter Tobin and Mrs. Lora Fogle

Dr. Walter L. Tobin
Interim Superintendent
Calhoun County Schools
and
Mrs. Lora A. Fogle
Regional Manager
PLATO Learning, Inc.

South Carolina continues to improve in teacher quality and is receiving positive national attention for the state level reforms in this area. New federal legislation encourages public and private partnerships, such as those developed through the CHEC Teacher Quality Enhancement Grant. This partnership included: the Community Higher Education Council (CHEC)-comprised of South Carolina State University, Claflin College and Orangeburg-Calhoun Technical College; the Local Education Agency (LEA) Partnership-comprised of Calhoun County Public Schools, Sumter School District Seventeen, Marion School District Seven, and Orangeburg Consolidated School Districts Three, Four and Five. PLATO Learning Inc. became an active partner by providing a web-based curriculum management solution designed to help connect the entire learning community. PLATO Orion provided tools to assist teachers and administrators in reaching accountability and student achievement goals. Utilizing Orion ensured that curriculum was aligned to state and local standards, and made it much easier for teachers to easily deliver this aligned curriculum to students.

There is much yet to be accomplished before every child in South Carolina has a qualified, competent classroom teacher. Partnerships such as those that began with the CHEC grant are important to this effort. Teachers must have the tools and resources necessary to provide standards-based instruction. Two major elements have been identified as key indicators in developing a successful standards-based reform model that affects positive change. First, district, as well as school-level leadership is needed to consistently support and encourage full integration of standards-based technology tools into the teaching and learning environment. Second, teachers and principals must engage in professional learning and planning that is standards-focused, ongoing, and is an intellectually vigorous part of their daily work.

Through a Teacher Quality Enhancement Grant, the Community Higher Education Council (CHEC) and Local Education Agency (LEA) Partnership set out to identify a teacher quality reform model for K-12 education. As part of the grant's objectives, CHEC sought to increase technology use in teaching, increase parental involvement, enhance leadership among principals and improve the education of K-12 learners, as well as pre-service and in-service teachers. CHEC chose NetSchools Orion by PLATO Learning, Inc., a web-based curriculum management solution designed to help connect the entire learning community. NetSchools Orion helps teachers reach accountability and student achievement goals by ensuring the curriculum is aligned to state and local standards, and offering tools to teachers to easily deliver this aligned curriculum to students. Teachers and students at the thirteen professional development schools in six districts began using NetSchools Orion during the first year of the CHEC Teacher Quality Enhancement Partnership.

NetSchools Partnership Donation Makes District Level Model Available

In year two and three of the grant, PLATO Learning proposed and initiated a Public/Private South Carolina Demonstration Project with CHEC, the six participating school districts, the South Carolina Governor's Office, and the South Carolina Association of School Administrators (SCASA), that would extend the reach of the grant to all schools in the participating districts, bringing the total number of schools being served to fifty. Including every school in the six districts provided the foundation to further develop the grant's technology goal, expand the partnership to a district-level, and promote a systemic reform model. Also key to the project was teacher and student access to NetSchools Orion, a train-the-trainer/capacity building model of consulting and professional development to ensure full implementation of the product throughout the schools and communities.

Funding Challenges

In year one, CHEC grant fully funded the technology initiative. In years two and three, PLATO Learning provided a more than two-to-one grant match, valued at over $1.4 million, showing full corporate commitment to the project. Each district was expected in return to provide full commitment and leadership. Instructional leaders across the six districts stepped up to the challenge and demonstrated their commitment. In the fourth year of the grant, districts were asked to contribute a matching portion in order to continue receiving funding from PLATO Learning and the CHEC grant. While all six districts initially indicated an interest to move forward, three districts (Calhoun County Public School, Orangeburg Consolidated School District Four, and Sumter School District 17) through determination, leadership, and vision, ultimately found funds necessary to take the initiative to the next level. PLATO Learning has proven its commitment to the partnership by continuing to support the grant-extending student and teacher subscriptions through year four (the 2002-2003 school year) with no year-four matching funds from the CHEC grant.

Example of a District Meeting Challenge

As Interim Superintendent of Calhoun County Public Schools, Dr. Walter L. Tobin saw going to the next level of implementation as a way of insuring that standards-based instruction was utilized by every teacher in every school in Calhoun County. However, initial usage reports indicated very few teachers were using NetSchools Orion regularly enough to make the changes in standards-based instruction that would result in adequate student progress, and school administrators were not using the tools the product offered to monitor lesson plans or benchmark testing. A closer look determined that teachers and administrators were not utilizing NetSchools Orion because they did not have proper access to the hardware needed to connect to the web-based application and tools. To remedy this situation, district staff devised a plan for each teacher to participate in training to help him or her utilize NetSchools Orion and use their new knowledge to build a bank of standards-based lesson plans. In addition, every teacher was given a new Internet-ready laptop to facilitate use at school and at home.

Improving Teacher Quality and Raising Academic Standards Continues to Be Focus

On-going evaluation and data collection will continue through the duration of the partnership. Thus far, two major elements have been identified as key indicators in developing a successful standards-based reform model that affects positive change. First, district, as well as school-level leadership is needed to consistently support and encourage full integration of standards-based technology tools into the teaching and learning environment. Second, teachers and principals must engage in professional learning and planning that is standards-focused, on going, and is an intellectually vigorous part of their daily work. While much still needs to be accomplished to assure that every child in South Carolina has a qualified, competent classroom teacher, South Carolina continues to improve in teacher quality. According to a national report card, Quality Counts 2003, published by *Education Week*, South Carolina is ranked "the best in the country" in the seventh annual report card on the state of school reform across the United States. South Carolina also ranked 12th nationally for raising academic standards.

Research Summary

Numerous research studies now demonstrate the power of professional development that focuses on reform:

- Professional development is more important than the computers (Sivin-Kachala and Bialo, 2002)
- Achievement gains are higher for students whose teachers have targeted reform-based professional development (Latham, 1999) and (Wenglinsky, 1980) (Wenglinsky, 2000 ETS and Milken Foundation)
- Professional development that is sustained and intense improves student achievement (National Education Goals Panel, 2000)
- Students improve when professional learning is given adequate time during the work day, and when professional development occurs through on-going processes such as workshops, guided peer observations with feedback, teacher collaborative groups, and demonstrated lessons by master teachers. (Learning First Alliance, Every Child Reading: A Professional Development Guide, 2000)

References

Richard, A. (2003). Quality Counts 2003-South Carolina State Profile, Bethesda, MD: Editorial Projects in Education, *Education Week*, 85-86.

Bialo, E. R. (1995). Report on the Effectiveness of Microcomputers in Schools, Washington, D.C. Software Publishers Assn.

Bialo, E. R. & J. Sivin-Kachala, (1995). Report on the Effectiveness of Technology in Schools '95–'96. Washington, D.C.: Software Publishers Assn.

Every Child Reading: A Professional Development Guide (2000). Baltimore, MD: The Learning Alliance-Association for Supervision and Curriculum Development.

Wurtz, E. (1998). The National Education Goals Panel. *National Education Goals: Lessons Learned, Challenges Ahead*, Washington, DC: Teachers College Record.

Wenglinsky, H. (200). *Report on How Teaching Matters; Bringing the Classroom Back Into Discussions of Teacher Quality.* Princeton, N.J.: Milken Family Foundation and Educational Testing Service.

Service-Learning: A Community Connection

Dr. Janice Belton Owens
Director, Clinical Experiences
School of Education
South Carolina State University
and
Dr. Helen Brantley
Professor, Teacher Education
South Carolina State University

(L - R) Dr. Janice Belton Owens, Mrs. Brenda Goodwin, Dr. Helen Brantley

Service learning activities can improve the knowledge, skills and dispositions of all educators and can help produce dramatic improvements in achievement in diverse and at-risk settings in the: school, home, centers and community. Personal, professional growth and connecting is an important community problem solver to create partnerships with agencies, organizations, and leaders. Community concerns and issues prepare the way to seek solutions and produce action to community barriers and growth. Reflective service learning projects can only enhance the goals and objectives of life-long community learners; thus, preparing them to become empowered politically, socially, educationally and economically.

Introduction

The National Council for Accreditation of Teacher Education (NCATE), is demanding that teacher preparation programs provide more varied opportunities for actual experiences with instructing and managing children and youth in a variety of contexts with increasing levels of complexity and challenges (NCATE, 2002). It is incumbent upon teacher education programs to integrate structured and deliberate service-learning activities across the curriculum. By implementing such practices, a community of learners striving toward a common mission is developed.

Additionally, service-learning provides unique and active opportunities to pre-service teachers to enhance and embellish teaching practices and beliefs (Ball, 1996) and assist in identifying and solving problems in the community. These experiences prepare teachers for a multiplicity of inter- and intra-agency collaboration, wholesome community connections, and quality partnerships. Additionally, the experience fosters sensitivity to diversity through first-hand community and field experiences (Chance, L., Morris, V. & Rakes, S., 1998).

A service-learning climate promotes growth of knowledge, skills and dispositions, as well as connects theory to practice. Pre-service teachers, who engage in service-learning, gain vicarious exposure to critical issues and community problems (Levesque & Posser, 1996). On the other hand, by working and receiving feedback from community mentors and coaches, they engage in making decisions and responding to human needs of diverse populations (Murtadha-Watts, 1998). Through this connection, broader world perspectives (Mahan & Stachowski, 1994), the bridge between theory and practice, humanistic and value education are realities. Pre-service teachers build on their humanistic spirit and construct their own knowledge about current issues and trends in context.

The School of Education Service-Learning Program

"David Imig, CEO and President of American Association of Colleges for Teachers Education (AACTE) says, "It's time to consider how service-learning can support unit accreditation efforts. It's time...because service-learning is an effective and efficient way for teacher candidates to demonstrate they are prepared to work in schools. It's time...because service-learning is sound pedagogical practice consistent with INTASC, state, and NCATE standards. It's time...because service-learning is the kind of community-based work that President George W. Bush and Senators Evan Bayh (D-IN) and John McCain (R-AZ) are advocating for Americans. It's time...because AACTE has the resources to help you incorporate service-learning into teacher education."

In aligning service-learning to a variety of field experiences and courses, the "humanistic practitioner" serves as the model in creating caring and civically responsible adults for pre-service teachers. The School of Education's conceptual framework emphasizes a need to transform humanistic teaching and learning in American schools so that it rests on an understanding of students, not only what they know but also how they think. This transformation calls for educating humanistic educators so they have a rich knowledge-base about learning and an array of tools for accessing student thinking, understanding students' prior knowledge and backgrounds and connecting to their families and communities (Darling-Hammond & Sclan, 1996).

Study of local-global connection leads to recognition that each of us makes choices that affect other people around the world, and others make choices that affect us. Because of this interconnectedness, global education includes knowledge and skills in decision-making, participation, and long-term involvement in the local community and in the larger world beyond our borders.

Students learn to find and process information from multiple humanistic perspectives (Alger& Harf, 1986).

During recent years, clinical programs have blended service-learning with the field-based education. Service-learning and other types of field education such as student teaching are all forms of experimental education. Service-learning involves blending the key elements of community services and internships so both the service providers and the service recipients benefit. These benefits result from a dual focus on the service being provided and the learning that will occur (Furco, 1996). Service-learning may be described as both a philosophy of education and an instructional method. As a philosophy of education, service-learning reflects the belief that education should develop social responsibility and prepare students to be involved citizens in democratic life. As an instructional method, service-learning involves a blending of service activities with the academic curriculum in order to address real community needs while students learn through active engagement. A growing body of research indicates that carefully planned and implemented service-learning projects can contribute to both K-12 students' and educators' learning and growth (Conrad & Hedin, 1991; Root, 1997).

Voices from the Service-Learning Experiences

Through service-learning teacher educators work with colleagues in other disciplines to identify academic coursework in the humanities, sciences, and social sciences so that undergraduate and graduate teachers have adequate foundational knowledge and in-service teachers have access to new, emerging real-life knowledge in their fields (Merryfield & Remy, 1995). Examples of service-learning experiences are illustrated in the following reflective journal excerpts from several pre-service teachers at South Carolina State University:

> **The experience provided me with hands-on and very worthwhile perspective of the role the community can play in the socialization process. When I went to my first community assignment, I was reluctant to express myself openly and freely concerning people with special needs. However, after assisting the Community Center Director with the activities for the evening, I relaxed and became interactive with the staff and residents. I discovered that they have the same dreams I have and enjoy some of the same activities. I thought of Maslow's hierarchy of needs and decided we are all the same; we just have different ways of showing it. The experience created a sense of compassion and love for teaching others from various backgrounds and experiences. Since that was my first day at the center, I often returned just to assist the director, who is also a good role model. I also play checkers with the residents. I help them out in other ways, such as going to the store and the local library so they can have time to use the Internet.*

> **The parents with whom I worked at the community center were elated that I could share strategies and suggestions with them on how to read a book with expression or*

> *how to provide advice to troubled teens. For example, I read stories to the community parents as well as acted many sections of the story. After I completed my readings and acting, the parents shared their ideas on how to use reading to motivate students at-risk. It is an excellent idea to read or have someone to read stories of interest to them. Along with the parents, we acted out many of the scenes. The parents asked if I could come to the community center in their building once a week and share my ideas. It was so nice to know that the parents saw worth in my dramatic spirit. I have returned several times just to assist in dramatizing the ideas we generated. These experiences have enlightened me about the community and dispelled many of the myths and misconceptions I had developed over the years. "I can say this was due to a lack of knowledge on my part." However, the experience with the parents, grandparents, and other neighborhood friends taught me lessons that are not available in university courses or classes. The community environment is enriched with talents and skills waiting to be tapped. I will always be community connected because the experience is very resourceful.*

> **I worked with the homeless for two years. It began as a class project. I now go for the pleasure of providing service. I truly believe it is my civic responsibility to give and to have concern for others. My service-learning experience has helped me to develop a caring and humanistic stance. As a pre-service teacher, I know I will be able to translate my activities in diverse class settings through many experiences. I will teach my K-8 students to engage in community service. I now see how character education skills can be taught through community service-learning.*

The journal excerpts reflect the need to align the training of teachers and other professional educators to the active participation and rich natural resource of the community. In his book, *Communities of Practice: Learning, Meaning, and Identity*, Wenger (1998) defines community as "the social configuration in which our enterprises are defined as worth pursuing and our participation is recognizable as competence" (p.5). The experiences that pre-service teachers have received through service-learning have significantly increased their ability to connect theory to the activities in the real world. The excerpts from the voices of the three pre-service teachers indicate the need to prepare and emphasize a caring and humanistic environment through a connection between service-learning and the community.

Cultivating a Service-Learning Climate

The School of Education at South Carolina State University and its school partners provide clinical and field-based experiences as integral components of the professional education curriculum. These experiences are designed to assist candidates in developing and demonstrating the knowledge, skills and dispositions necessary to help all students learn. Prospective educators (teachers, counselors, speech therapists, and administrators) are provided an array of opportunities to interact with P-12 culturally diverse and exceptional children throughout forty-six (46) school districts in the partnership consortium.

Under the supervision of K-12, national board certified, master teachers, and professional education faculty, teacher education candidates actively participate with families, schools and communities through a variety of course activities, action research and reflective assignments. The objective is to provide sequentially planned clinical and field experiences which will prepare educators who are reflective decision makers, and effective performers in a diverse technological society.

Candidates enrolled in basic undergraduate programs complete a minimum of one-hundred-fifty (150) clock hours of sequential and incremental clinical, field-based, and service experiences prior to their capstone field experiences, student teaching. Prospective graduate candidates complete a minimum of fifty (50) clock-hours of such experiences prior to enrolling in the practicum and/or internship capstone semester.

Intensive service-learning and community assignments are significant parts of the out-of-classroom experiences. Courses in foundations, technology, and methods help undergraduate and graduate educators examine conceptualizations, cases, instructional strategies, curriculum development, interdisciplinary approaches, and assessments in global education and diversity through service and community learning. Research courses include relevant studies, literature, and opportunities for action research, and set aside time for educators to reflect, experiment, and share ideas and experiences with colleagues (Merryfield, 1995; Tye & Tye, 1992).

Undergraduate and graduate educators cite the following reasons for integrating field experiences/service-learning into their courses: (1) to prepare new teachers and up-grade the skills of veteran teachers to use service-learning as a teaching method with their K-12 students; (2) to help socialize all teachers, administrators and service providers in the essential moral and civic engagement, adapting to the needs of learners with diverse and special needs, and having to commit to advocate for social justice for children and families; (3) to enhance all educators' ability to reflect critically on current educational practices and their own teaching; (4) to develop in all educators the dispositions and abilities needed to easily and fully adopt other educational reforms such as authentic assessment, teaching with integrated thematic units, focusing on higher order thinking skills, and making improvements in school schedules and climate; (5) to accelerate the process of learning how to perform a variety of roles needed to meet the needs of students such as counselor, community liaison advocate, and moral leader; and (6) to develop human service-oriented professionals who can work effectively in schools with integrated services or other social service settings with students from diverse backgrounds.

References

Ball, D.L (1996). Teacher learning and the mathematics reforms: What we think we know and what we need to learn. *Phi Delta Kappan*, 77(7), 500-508.

Chance, L., Morris, V,. & Rakes, S. (1998). Fostering Sensitivity to diverse cultures through an early field experience collaborative. *Journal of Teacher Education*, 47(5), 386-389.

Darling-Hammond, L., & Sclan, E. (1996). Policy and supervision yearbook: Association for Supervision and Curriculum Development. Alexandria, VA.

Levesque, J., & Prosser, T. (1996). service-learning connections. *Journal of Teacher Education*, 47(5), 325-334.

Tye, B.B., & Tye, K.A. (1992). *Global education – A study of school change.* State University of New York Press.

Merryfield, M., & Remy, R.L. (1995). *Teaching about international conflict and peace.* New York.

Wenger, E. (1998). *Communities of practice: Learning, meaning, and identity.* Cambridge University Press.

Recruitment and Retention of Teachers – A Teaching Fellows Program

(L - R) Dr. Caroletta Shuler, Dr. Jesse Kinard

Dr. Jesse E. Kinard
Chair, Department of Teacher Education
South Carolina State University
and
Dr. Caroletta A. Shuler
Assistant Professor, School of Education
South Carolina State University

The challenge to recruit and retain teachers for our schools is a state and national priority. However, inadequate salaries, numerous accelerated standards through increased testing, inadequate working environments, and early teacher attrition are some of the obstacles that affect the recruitment and availability of teachers throughout the nation. Moreover, data show that these obstacles adversely affect minority teachers. Producing an adequate pool of high qualified teachers is the main goal of Teaching Fellows Program. This program aims to achieve this goal by combining the knowledge base, ethics, vision, and the students' positive attitudes along with their educational experience. Teaching Fellows participate in activities that complement their unique and challenging educational experience at South Carolina State University. There are currently 21 students of color participating in the program.

Introduction

America's teacher recruitment and retention challenge has been well documented and widely reported in the literature and national media (Darling-Hammond, Dilworth, and Bullmaster, 1996; Brown, Hughes, and Vance, 1999; Eubanks and Weaver, 1999; Chronister, 2000). Urban and rural schools, particularly in impoverished communities, are finding it harder to find and keep qualified teachers (Eubanks and Weaver, 1999). Likewise, while the public school student population is currently 34.5% minority and is projected to be over 50% by 2035 (U.S. Department of Commerce, 1996), the public school teacher population remains overwhelmingly white, with only 13.5% teachers of color (National Center for Education Statistics, 2001). The Teaching Fellows Program at South Carolina State University builds a greater awareness of the social context of schools in South Carolina and ensures that there will be a larger pool of quality teachers for all students.

Various "grow-your-own" strategies have been implemented, and offer incentives to local residents to become teachers. According to Collins (1999), colleges must take a greater role in recruiting high-caliber students with the potential to become successful teachers. A teacher's involvement in community, educational and cultural programs influences the decision to stay or leave. Therefore, recruitment and retention of teachers require a coordinated school-community effort. State programs for recruiting and retaining teachers vary widely and include equalized teacher salaries, teacher supply-and-demand analyses by subject area and community, teacher placement clearinghouses, scholarships and loans, advertising in other targeted states, forgiving student loans for years of teacher service, and related career activities for secondary students (Collins, 1999)

In 1999, the South Carolina General Assembly recognized the shortage of teachers in this state and funded the Teaching Fellows Program for South Carolina. The mission of the South Carolina Teaching Fellows Program is to recruit talented high school seniors into the teaching profession and to help them develop leadership qualities. Each year, the program provides fellowships for up to 200 high school seniors who have exhibited high academic achievement, a history of service to the school and community, and a desire to teach South Carolina's children (South Carolina Center for Teacher Recruitment, 2003).

Review of Literature

Some people define good teachers as those who are certified. A "highly qualified teacher in every classroom" is their mantra. However, are certified teachers actually better teachers? Proponents of another school of thought argue that great teaching has very little, if anything, to do with certification or methodology courses, but rather with knowledge in one or more content areas, passion about one's subject, and love for children (Hammond, 1994). "High quality" (vs. "highly qualified") teachers are what this group proposes. High quality means (at least at the middle school and secondary school levels) teachers who have a degree in the discipline they teach (mathematics, science, history, foreign language, literature, the arts, and the like), preferably from a liberal arts college with competitive admissions criteria. These teachers also have life experiences that enrich the teaching itself. The idea here is that one needs to know something deeply to teach it well, and to care about it to teach it passionately. It's easier to help new teachers learn *how* to teach well–using strong mentoring systems, than to teach them *what* to teach (Bassett, 2003).

So what characteristics determine teacher quality? According to Bassett (2003), using a meta-analysis of the available research, the Abell Foundation determined that verbal ability and the selectivity of the college the teacher attended are the key factors in teacher quality. The U.S. Department of

Education's 2002 report "Meeting the Highly Qualified Teachers Challenge: The Secretary's Annual Report on Teacher Quality" concurs. "Studies have consistently documented the important connection between a teacher's verbal and cognitive abilities and student achievement." The report states that adding "subject-matter background can also have a positive effect on student performance." Thus, schools with high-achieving students tend to be those where the teachers have a deep knowledge base about the subjects they are teaching, where the teachers were themselves high-performing students in high school and college, where the teachers are impassioned about their subjects, and where the teachers care about the children they teach (Bassett, 2003).

South Carolina State University Teaching Fellows Program

The mission of the South Carolina State University (SCSU) Teaching Fellows Program is to prepare pre-service educators through a variety of academic and cultural experiences that enhance leadership and professionalism. The University's School of Education's Teacher Education Program is a rigorous program aligned with high standards and nationally accredited by NCATE. All teacher education graduates meet state accreditation requirements. In addition, the program features enrichment experiences such as leadership development; seminars which focus on interpersonal and team building skills; seminars which focus on relevant and timely educational issues and trends; cultural activities and workshops; opportunities to study aboard; early field experiences in PK-12 schools; and teacher certification for the state of South Carolina. Teaching Fellows benefit from the guidance offered by School of Education faculty and PK-12 master teachers as mentors. Teaching Fellows who meet the requirement may also participate in the University's Honors Program.

The University's Teaching Fellows Programs goals are: 1) to provide an academically and culturally enriched preparation program that extends beyond the regular university program; 2) to provide opportunities and experiences that encourage the development of leaders and decision-makers; 3) to provide opportunities for building an understanding of the place of education in a greater social context; 4) to promote a sense of mission, service and professionalism; and 5) to recruit and retain a greater number of male and minority teacher education candidates.

Teaching Fellows explore various issues related to interest groups formation and articulation, the politics of school decision-making, how policies are implemented, and other issues affecting policy. Teaching Fellows also take field trips to the South Carolina General Assembly to observe legislation in the making. Teaching Fellows, as well as all teacher candidates at South

Carolina State University, learn about professional ethics within the classroom with students, parents, colleagues, and administrators. A quality teacher should always adhere to the correct conduct about teaching by using the National Education Association, the state, or the school district's Code of Ethics.

Teaching Fellows have had professional development training since their freshman year by participating in the South Carolina Black Caucus Alliance Seminars. This experience allows them to meet and speak one-on-one with state legislators about the state of education in South Carolina. South Carolina State University's Teaching Fellows (2000 Cohort) also participated in the 2002 *Energy Educators Seminar for South Carolina Teaching Fellows* sponsored by Santee Cooper. Fellows received training in energy education, in aquaculture, in training employees in an industry and how industry and local schools can cooperate to improve the community, environmental educational training, and in electrical education training. Fellows were required to produce lesson plans based on what they have learned and to incorporate that knowledge base to their prospective majors.

SCSU Teaching Fellows have presented at Special Education Conferences to Teaching Cadets, student teachers, and inservice special educators. Teaching Fellows have provided seminars and workshops to Teacher Cadets such as Seamless Education from 12th grade to College, dressing for success, and selecting the best college for you. Teaching Fellows also perform varied community services, such as tutoring in school, in districts as PACT Academy tutors, and by working with at-risk children in a variety of settings outside of the classroom.

Becoming a certified teacher requires graduates to complete an approved program of study and successfully pass the PRAXIS I and PRAXIS II in the state of South Carolina. Teaching Fellow Matthew Owens has the distinction of successfully passing the PRAXIS I and II in his freshman year at South Carolina State University as a mathematics education major. These accomplishments were possible due to his enrollment in summer sessions, strong work ethics, dedication and a blend of a unique personal "fiber." Matthew will be the first Teaching Fellow to graduate in the state in three years since the program's implementation by the SC General Assembly.

South Carolina State University's Teaching Fellows (2000 Cohort) who currently are juniors with senior hours at the institution must complete 300 - 400 contact Pre-STEP hours with children in public schools and community service prior to student teaching. The majority of their pre-clinical experience hours are under the supervision of National Board Certified teachers in their respective areas of study. All the 2000 Cohort of Teaching Fellows are trained to teach based on their areas standards and the state of SC standards.

Conclusion

Teaching Fellows, who are considered advanced teacher candidates at South Carolina State University, must demonstrate a knowledge base. They are given the opportunity to practice their skills and convey their knowledge by participating at conferences, in workshops, and in classroom settings with children and inservice teachers. This allows them to observe educational training in environments such as learning math via the ALCOA Company, and teaching science via aquaculture. Energy education and environmental education teach them that education is not just within the classroom setting. Teaching Fellows must learn to integrate various subjects to particular fields of study, e.g., early childhood education, elementary education, math education, and speech pathology and audiology.

South Carolina State University's philosophy is, "It takes a dedicated university with focused programs to prepare highly knowledgeable and skillful teachers for the nation's schools." Based on the review of the literature and the combined experience of both authors of this article (35 years), it is vital that the recruitment and retention of teachers must have program components with involvement and commitment. Recruiting, preparing and retaining good teachers are at the heart of the University's Teaching Fellows Program. In addition, the goal of attracting the best and brightest to the profession involves the total collaboration of several components. Components such as community leaders, ministers/clergy, business/corporations, educators and parents must collaborate in response to our nation's priority challenge - the recruitment and retention of high quality teachers.

References

Bassett, P. (2003). Searching for great teachers. Education Week, 22(24), 26,28.

Brown, J.W., Hughes, G.B., & Vance, P.L. (1999). The new face of teaching in the 21st century: Are we ready for the challenge? *The Journal of Negro Education*, 68(3), 241-244.

Chronister, G. (Ed.). (2000). Who should teach? Quality Counts 2000. Education Week, 19(18).

Darling-Hammond, L., Dilworth, M.E., & Bullmaster, M. (1996). Educators of color (Commissioned Paper). Washington, D.C.: Office of Educational Research and Improvement (OERI), U.S. Department of Education.

Eubanks, S.C., & Weaver, R. (1999). Excellence through diversity: Connecting the teacher quality and teacher diversity agendas. *The Journal of Negro Education*, 68(3), 451-459.

Darling-Hammond, L., (2001). Standards For Teachers, 34th Charles W. Hunt, Lecture.

National Center for Educational Statistics, (2001). Digest of Education Statistics (NCES 2001-034). Washington, DC: Office of Educational Research and Improvement, U.S. Department of Education.

South Carolina Center for Teacher Recruitment, (2003). South Carolina Teaching Fellows. Columbia, SC: South Carolina Center for Teacher Recruitment.

U.S. Department of Commerce, (1996). Current population reports: Population projections of the United States by age, sex, race, and Hispanic origin, 1995 to 2050. Washington, DC: U.S. Department of Commerce.

Project Blossom and Service-Learning

Dr. BerNadette Lawson-Williams
Assistant Professor
Department of Health and Physical Education
Johnson C. Smith University

During the 2002 fall semester, Project Blossom, an afterschool physical activity and mentoring program for female adolescents in Orangeburg, S.C., was implemented in the Department of Health and Physical Education at South Carolina State University. The primary goal of this program was to provide teacher candidates majoring in physical education an opportunity to acquire, apply, and strengthen their professional skills in a realistic physical activity setting.

Introduction

Empowering teacher candidates to become "Effective performers, reflective decision makers, and humanistic practitioners" through physical and activity service learning experiences.

The benefits of service learning activities for all can be rewarding for schools, communities and institution of higher learning. Cutforth (2000) defines service learning as a teaching strategy that provides students with the opportunity to acquire academic, social, career, and personal skills through their involvement in community service projects. Service learning is significant because of its implications for stimulating a transition toward healthier and mutually beneficial campus-community partnerships (Zlotkowski, 1996). Consistent with South Carolina State University's (SCSU) School of Education theme, "The Professional Educator as an Effective Performer, Reflective Decision Maker, and Humanistic Practitioner," the Department of Health and Physical Education strongly emphasizes the importance of service learning experiences in fostering the personal and professional growth of its teacher candidates. During the 2002 fall semester, an afterschool physical activity and mentoring program for underprivileged and inactive female adolescents in Orangeburg, S.C., called Project Blossom was coordinated by Dr. BerNadette Lawson-Williams. This program awarded numerous opportunities for teacher candidates to acquire practical experiences working in a physical activity setting.

Despite the number of sport opportunities available for women and girls since the passage of Title IX in 1975, female adolescents remain the least active segment in the American population (U. S. Department of Health and Human Services, 1996). The primary goal of Project Blossom was to provide positive opportunities for underprivileged adolescent females to engage in physical activities that would foster their physical, emotional, intellectual, and social growth. The purpose of this article is to describe the components of Project Blossom, along with the program's impact on the personal and professional development of South Carolina State University and its teacher education candidates.

Project Description

Project Blossom was supported by the Kellogg Foundation's South Carolina Leadership in Public Service Mini Grant Program. The goals of Project Blossom were: to allow college female students to serve as positive role models for adolescent female students; to provide students majoring in physical education an opportunity to acquire, apply, and strengthen their professional skills in a variety of realistic physical activity settings; to provide opportunities for inactive and underprivileged adolescent females in Orangeburg, S.C., to become exposed to physical activity in a friendly and socially conducive environment; to foster and promote the necessity of establishing partnerships between teacher candidates and in-service teachers in Orangeburg, S.C., schools; to strengthen the relationship between university and community personnel; and to emphasize the importance of service learning projects in the development of more competent and experienced teacher candidates.

Organization

Prior to selecting program participants for the Project Blossom, numerous female students majoring in physical education were identified to serve as staff members. As staff members, their duties entailed planning, organizing and executing all aspects of the program's activities. Students interested in applying for staff positions submitted applications, completed waiver forms, and participated in interviews. Six students were selected for the interview process, ranging in classification from sophomore to senior. These individuals were selected based on their involvement in community activities, interest in working with female adolescents, their knowledge of sport and fitness concepts, and their ability to develop a positive relationship with program participants, and their service with positive role models.

Three positions were created to identify job responsibilities: a senior project coordinator, a junior coordinator, and project counselors. The six students selected for the program were assigned to the specific positions based on their experience and knowledge in the areas of project management, supervision and leadership. One student was selected to serve as the senior coordinator. In this capacity, she was responsible for facilitating the project, including supervising other staff members, conducting program evaluations; assisting in the preparation of healthy snacks for program participants, and performing other tasks as assigned by the project coordinator. Another student was selected for the junior coordinator position. Her duties entailed selecting daily program activities, distributing equipment and session materials to participants, creating and maintaining program participants' attendance and behavior logs, and executing other tasks as assigned by the senior coordinator. The four remaining students were selected as project counselors. Their primary responsibilities included organizing and implementing warm-up, stretch, and cooperative activities, facilitating discussion sessions, distributing healthy snacks, and other tasks assigned by the senior and junior coordinators.

Implementation

Project Blossom was not only designed to promote the importance of physical activity to inactive and underprivileged adolescent females in grades 6-8, but also emphasized the importance of providing a learning environment conducive to socialization. Once funding was established from the South Carolina Leadership in Public Service Mini Grant Program, Howard Middle School was contacted for collaborative opportunities. Howard Middle School, located in Orangeburg, South Carolina, was targeted for this project because of its large population of at-risk students. Once the partnership was established, the school's counselor identified 30 prospective participants based on their school attendance, discipline, and academic records. These students were required to return several consent forms to participate in the program. Of the 30 students identified, fifteen returned the appropriate forms required for program participation.

Project Blossom was for three months, October through December. A total of nine sessions were held for two and a half hours. All project sessions included warm-up, stretch, and cool down activities, fitness and cooperative games, and a discussion activity, which provided the participants with an opportunity to express their concerns pertaining to personal topics such as peer pressure, body image, and self-esteem. The discussion activity also allowed Project Blossom staff members to interact with program participants, share their personal experiences, and introduce various topics, including career goals, stress management, eating disorders, developing communication skills, proper study habits, and the importance of maintaining a healthy lifestyle through physical activity.

Participants were exposed to 14 sport activities, including tennis, golf, soccer, basketball, badminton, flag football, dance, relay races, tug-of-war, circuit training, volleyball, bowling, fitness quiz bowls, and cheerleading. Other program activities included field trips to an SCSU football game, a local roller-skating rink, and Edisto Gardens. Students also toured SCSU 's campus and received a surprise visit from Miss SCSU. All participants enjoyed healthy snacks following program sessions and received physical activity posters, workbooks, and other educational wellness materials. At the conclusion of the program, an awards ceremony was held to recognize the hard work, dedication, and accomplishments of all participants. Participants received trophies, achievement plaques, participation certificates, and SCSU paraphernalia.

Evaluation

Project Blossom participants were required to take a pre-test, which was administered during the first program session and a post-test, which was administered during the last program session. The pre-test was utilized to assess the participants' attitudes and behaviors towards exercising, along with their knowledge of wellness concepts before participating in the program. The post-test was used to measure any changes that may have occurred in the participants' attitudes and behaviors, along with knowledge gained of wellness concepts following the completion of the program. During the evaluation plan, program participants were randomly selected to participate in a videotaped interview. The feedback gained from the interview determined the program's effectiveness in helping its participants achieve their personal wellness goals. The data was also utilized to evaluate staff personnel, activity selection, and program session frequency and duration.

According to the post-test, Project Blossom was effective in helping participants increase their knowledge of various sport and types of physical activities, gain self-confidence, and improve social skills. Upon the completion of this project, program participants blossomed into individuals who realized and appreciated the benefits of being physically active, along with making wise and healthy life choices.

Reflection

The success of Project Blossom was due primarily to its staff. For ten weeks, these students worked diligently to organize, plan, implement, and manage the project. However, most impressive was their ability to develop healthy and nurturing relationships with program participants. Following the conclusion of the program, staff members were required to evaluate their effectiveness in accomplishing the project's goals, along with identifying the professional skills that they utilized, developed, strengthened, or felt needed improvement.

Staff evaluations of the program are as follows:

- "Working with Project Blossom was a wonderful experience. The program gave me the opportunity to share my experiences with the participants. I would recommend this program to future participants and staff members because it serves as an opportunity to allow college students to interact with middle school students, in which both entities can learn and benefit from the other." (Shayla Williams, Student Counselor, Senior)
- "My experience working with Project Blossom was a great one which made me realize how much I enjoy working with children. During the allotted time each Wednesday, I was able to work with the participants as a group and on a one on one basis. I would recommend this program to prospective staff members because it is a great chance to become a role model and help young children." (Yolanda Gray, Student Counselor, Junior)
- "In working with Project Blossom, I became more aware of the skills that I possess as a leader. I learned that a lot goes into developing and managing sport and physical education programs. It was an enjoyable program and I gained substantial knowledge about myself." (Shaniqua Simmons, Junior Coordinator, Senior)
- "My experiences working with Project Blossom were positive. Prior to my participation in the project, I was a very shy and timid person, but the program helped me overcome that shyness. I learned that I could actually get in front of people and teach a lesson without being too nervous." (Nikiyah Spearman, Student Counselor, Junior)
- "My experience working with the program was very enlightening. This experience influenced my career goals and will make me more marketable. I would recommend this program to prospective staff members because of the benefit of learning about nutrition, various sports, and gaining more knowledge about the personalities of adolescent females." (Vershion Funderburk, Senior Coordinator, Senior)
- "My experience working with Project Blossom gave me hands on experience and made me realize that I really want to be a physical education teacher. This program also taught me patience and that I can do anything that I want to do." (Alicia Willoughby, Student Counselor, Sophomore)

Conclusion

While this service- learning experience provided teacher candidates an opportunity to enhance their professional skills, it also allowed them the opportunity to apply classroom concepts in a practical setting, thereby promoting the development of the knowledge, skills, and cognitive capacities necessary for students to deal effectively with the complex social issues that challenge citizens (Eyler, 2002). As observed through Project Blossom, service-learning allows students to become involved in the community outside of school in a way that not only expands the learning process but also brings them closer to real-life problems and potential solutions. This method of learning involves much more than simply retaining information or practicing skills. Students are forced to adapt their knowledge and skills and utilize them to solve the problems at hand (Arellano-Unruh and Moorman, 2002). This process ultimately results in a teacher candidate who is empowered to become a "professional educator, effective performer, reflective decision maker, and humanistic practitioner."

References

Arellano-Unruh, N., & Moorman, M. (2002). Community service-learning projects for under graduate recreation majors. *Journal of Physical Education*, Recreation & Dance, 73(2) 42-47.

Cutforth, N. (2000). Connecting school physical education to the community through service learning. *Journal of Physical Education*, Recreation & Dance, 71(2) 39.

Eyler, J. (2002). Reflection: linking service and learning–linking students and communities. *Journal of Social Issues*, 58(3) 517-525.

U. S. Department of Health and Human Services. (1996). Physical activity and health: A report of the Surgeon General. Atlanta, GA: Centers for Disease Control and Prevention.

Zlotkowski, E. (1996). A new voice at the table? Linking service learning and the academy. *Change*, 28(1) 20-27.

Project FLAVA

Dr. Martha Jean Adams-Heggins
Professor, Teacher Education
South Carolina State University
and Director, Project FLAVA

Higher education is an essential part of the complicated equation needed to address the issue of youth violence in America/the world during this Post Modern Era. The article written by Dr. Martha Jean Adams-Heggins describes a research demonstration program at SCSU, which is based on the Family Community and Violence Prevention (FCVP) Model. To date, more than 24 colleges and universities located in 17 states, the District of Columbia, and the U.S. Virgin Islands have successfully implemented the FCVP Model. Evaluation data to date clearly substantiate that FCVP Programs demonstrate significant effects in the behavior and academic achievement of "at risk" youth served by its nationwide system of Family Life Centers. South Carolina State University Family Life Center is sponsored by SCSU in a cooperative agreement with Central State University (CSU), Wilberforce, Ohio, the Office of Minority Health, and the U.S. Department of Health and Human Services.

South Carolina State University Family Life Center – Project FLAVA Program: A Model for Violence Prevention in Higher Education

Building trust and peace by acknowledging and celebrating the sacredness of cultural diversity and contributing to the empowerment of our communities, the FCVP Program will create a culture of civility that serves as a foundation for empowering children and families to maintain a secure, safe, and nurturing environment. (FCVP Vision Statement, 2002)

South Carolina State University Family Life Center - Project FLAVA (SCSU FLC) is sponsored by SCSU in a cooperative agreement with Central State University's Family and Community Violence Prevention Program (CSU-FCVP), the Office of Minority Health, and the Department of Health and Human Services. The purpose of FCVP is to positively impact the academic and personal development of a select group of children and youth who are at risk for involvement in violent and other abusive behaviors.

The number of Americans who have been victimized by violent crime is staggering. Between 1990 - 1994, the number of people murdered in our country (119,732) was 58,000 - more than twice the number killed in the

Vietnam War (Bennett, 1996). In 1994 alone, 10.8 million Americans were the victims of violent crime, more than twice the number injured in motor vehicle accidents (Bennett, 1996). According to a US Department of Justice report in 1994, twenty-three percent (23%) of all households had been victimized by crime. Juvenile offenders were responsible for fourteen percent (14%) of all violent crimes and twenty-five percent (25%) of all property crimes. Two million seven hundred thousand (2,700,000) juveniles were arrested, more than a third under the age of fifteen (US Department of Justice, 1996).

Each year, the Children's Defense Fund publishes a yearbook entitled *The State of America's Children.* According to their 2000 issue, children under age fifteen in the US compared to children in twenty-five other industrialized countries combined are: 1) 12 times more likely to die from gunfire; 2) 16 more times likely t o murder with a gun; 3) 11 times more likely to commit suicide with a gun; and 4) 9 times more likely to die in a firearm accident.

Furthermore, based on a recent article by (Toppo, 2003) school violence has now hit the lower grades e.g. kindergarten, first, second, etc. Specifically, throughout the nation, elementary school principals and safety experts are reporting more violence and aggression in even the youngest students. Subsequently, these school leaders and safety experts are blaming parents, prenatal medical problems, and an angry society, etc. as part of the reasons (USA Today, January 13, 2003). These data strongly suggest that there is a critical need to address violence/crime in society. To this end, many are asking these questions: How many more children will have to die before we say enough is enough and address the issue of violence? How many more children will "kill" before they learn to "read" and/or "reason"? How many more children will be "robbed" of their "childhood" and "adolescence"? How many more children will pass school and fail life? How long will we continue to fail our children by not implementing violence prevention programs, models, and strategies in the homes, school, and community?

To address the aforementioned problems, issues, and concerns, South Carolina State University has taken the leadership in the community of Orangeburg, South Carolina to establish a Family and Community Violence Prevention (FCVP) Program for at-risk children and families. SCSU FLC - Project FLAVA is a research demonstration project designed for high risk/at risk children, youth, and families who reside in the Sprinkle community, i.e. the lowest educational and income area in Orangeburg, South Carolina. Pre and Post-tests are administered to participants utilizing several state and national standardized tests, including, but not limited to the WRAT and PACT tests. Thus, Pretest results are used to guide and facilitate growth in the academic and personal development areas throughout the program year.

The objectives of Project FLAVA are: 1) To identify, recruit, and select 60 participants from the Sprinkle community; 2) to demonstrate a minimum of 20% improvement in reading, spelling, and mathematics; 3) to demonstrate a minimum of 20% participants in participant's school bonding; 4) to demonstrate a 20% increase in family bonding activities; 5) to demonstrate a minimum of 20% increase in parent involvement and parent education; 6) to demonstrate a 30% increase in socialization, social competence, and school adjustment; 7) to increase violence prevention, peace education concepts, and life management skills by 20%; 8) to demonstrate a 20% increase level of openness and tolerance toward cultural differences; 9) to demonstrate a 30% positive affiliation for one's own ethnic group; 10) to increase participant involvement in wholesome recreational/leisure activities by 30%; 11) to increase family involvement in wholesome recreational/leisure activities by 30%; and 12) to demonstrate a 30% increase in career awareness.

Selection (priority) is given to participants that show three to five risk factors: 1) suspension from school; 2) high employment of parents; 3) alcohol and other drug use/abuse in the home; 4) high level of delinquency; 5) limited access to social services by youth and family; 6) physical and emotional (behavioral); 7) low academic performances; 8) low educational achievement of parents/guardians; 9) single parent household, etc. Sixty (60) elementary and middle school children were recruited for the 2002 - 2003 Program Year.

FLAVA provides the conceptual framework that links key stakeholders with the community: a) parental and family support; b) the schools/universities; c) the government; d) the culture community; e) the social and business entities; f) law enforcement, and the ministerial alliances, etc. The theme of Project FLAVA is Breaking the Cycle of Violence: Mind, Body, and Spirit. FLAVA has established numerous partnerships with organizations/agencies on SCSU campus and in the community. Namely: a) The School of Education, b) Felton Laboratory School, c) The Community Higher Education Council - Local Education Agencies Teacher Quality Enhancement Partnership (CHEC-LEA), d) Mellichamp Elementary School, e) Orangeburg Area Development Center, f) The Department of Military Sciences, g) The Department of Human Services, h) The Department of Social Work, I) Henderson Davis Theatre/Dr. Frank M. Mundy, Director, j) Athletic Department k) Ujimaa Dance Company and/or Riverbank School of Ethnic Dance l)Orangeburg Consolidated School District #5.

Each FCVP is required to develop curricula in each of the following components: a) Academic Development; b) Personal Development; c) Cultural Development; d) Career Development; e) Recreational Enrichment; and f) Family Bonding, etc. Thus, SCSU FLC has written and/or adopted curricula for each of the major components: a) academic, personal, cultural, and career development.

To date, five thematic units have been written. The three thematic units in the Personal Development area are entitled: a) Personal Development: I Am a Great Somebody; b) Conflict Resolution: Everyone's Responsibility; and c) Peace Education: Let There Be Peace and Let It Begin With Me. The two thematic units that were written in the Culture Enrichment Component are: a) "Kwanzaa: A Celebration of Family, Community and Culture, and b) "Teaching Cultural Awareness Through Literature: An African American Perspective." And, the unit title for the Career Development component is, "Career Awareness: Will You Be Able to Afford Your Nikes?" We are especially pleased with these thematic units/curricula because they are age, grade, and developmentally appropriate for the participants we serve. Additionally, FLAVA has adopted an academic curriculum that has been correlated to address the PACT test in South Carolina for grades third through fifth. Likewise, programs for the Family Bonding and Mentoring components have been written and implemented. Finally, the Conceptual Framework for SCSU FLC Program has been written.

Project FLAVA office is housed on the campus of SCSU University; and the Afterschool Program is housed in Mellichamp Elementary School; Monday, Wednesday, and Thursday from 3:00 – 6:00pm and Tuesday from 1:30pm to 6:00pm. Additional family bonding activities and the recreation program (Saturday Academy) are held twice a month at the Orangeburg Area Development Center (located in the Sprinkle Community) from 9:00 – 2:00pm. The 2002 – 2003 program year began September 30, 2002.

Through the aforementioned conceptual framework, Project FLAVA utilizes curricula models for violence prevention that match the real problems in the community. Furthermore, curricula for the Family Life Center is based on "Best Practices" using cognitive, affective, and psychomotor domain research, informed opinions, and sound pedagogy.

An analysis of the WRAT Pretest Data showed that the majority of the participants were at the third grade level in language arts, i.e. spelling. Likewise, the data showed that the majority of the participants were at the third grade level in mathematics. These data are consistent with the results of the PACT test results that show the majority of Project FLAVA participants in the fifth grade are at the third grade level in reading and mathematics. Therefore, as veteran educators, researchers, and scholars the following hypotheses are made: a) that the objectives of the program will be met; and b) that there will be a substantial improvement in the academic and personal development of FLAVA's participants as measured by the Posttest assessments.

The FCVP goal/vision is that by 2010, the FCVP will be the most effective program demonstrating the reduction and/or prevention of violence among at risk minority children and youth in Orangeburg, South Carolina and throughout the nation. Likewise, SCSU FLC will be a model for teaching about violence prevention programs in higher education. For additional information see www.scsu.edu/flava.

References:

Bennett, W.J., DeJulio, J.J., Jr., & Walters, J.P. (1996). *Body Count: Moral Poverty...and How to Win America's War Against Crime and Drugs.* Simon & Schuster: New York.

Toppo, G. (2003). School Violence Hits Lower Grades. *USA Today.*

U.S. Department of Justice 1996. Victim's Report 9% Fewer Crimes Last Year. Press Release: Washington, D.C.

The Children's Defense Fund. *The State of America's Children Yearbook 2000.* Washington, D.C.

The Role of Two-Year Colleges in Preparing Teachers

Dr. Anne Crook, President
Orangeburg Calhoun Technical College
and
Mike Hammond
Vice President for Administration

(L – R) Mike Hammond, Dr. Anne Crook

All segments of higher education must collaborate to prepare highly qualified individuals to meet the challenge of a national shortage of 2.4 million teachers. Three institutions of higher education in Orangeburg, South Carolina – Claflin University, South Carolina State University, and Orangeburg-Calhoun Technical College – joined together in 1996 as the Community Higher Education Council (CHEC) to help address this task.

These schools have successfully collaborated to make the following enhancements to public education in the state: 1) Recruited candidates for teacher education; 2) provided technology training to current teachers; 3) provided student tutors to area schools; 4) increased the number of National Board Certified teachers; and 5) increased the number of teachers with advanced degrees.

Dealing with this major nationwide teacher shortage is a serious problem mandating innovative solutions from higher education. The CHEC partnership has shown the potential for two-year institutions to be a force in providing highly-qualified teachers to meet the needs of the nation.

Facing a national teacher shortage of 2.4 million, the challenge of preparing "highly qualified" teachers for public schools must become a shared task of all segments of higher education. The newest player in preparing teachers is the two-year college. The first national conference of two-year college teacher education programs –"Blazing the Trail, Pioneering Community College Teacher Education Programs" – met in Phoenix, Arizona, in March 2003. At least 20 states have made progress in the development of teacher education programs in two-year institutions.

In South Carolina, there are sixteen two-year technical colleges under the South Carolina Technical College System. The South Carolina Commission of Higher Education has worked to forge together a list of seventy-four transfer courses that students may take from the sixteen technical colleges to the public four-year institutions. However, there are no recognized teacher education programs at the two-year level. Various articulation models have been worked out between specific technical colleges and their four-year partners.

The two-year institutions in South Carolina offer Associate Degrees in Arts and Science, as well as the Associate Degree in Early Child Care and Education. The latter degree was developed specifically for persons preparing to be employed at childcare centers and to work as Head Start Directors. Some individual technical colleges have entered into articulation agreements with local institutions of higher education to provide a seamless pathway, i.e., "2 + 2" agreement in Early Childhood Education with SCSU's School of Education.

In Orangeburg, South Carolina, there are three institutions of higher education – Claflin University, South Carolina State University, and Orangeburg-Calhoun Technical College. These institutions joined together in 1996 as the Community Higher Education Council (CHEC). In 1999, the CHEC partnership received a Title II CHEC/LEA Teacher Quality Enhancement Partnership Grant, with one of its goals being to enhance teacher education programs in the region.

Working closely together, the collaboration has successfully made the following achievements to enhance public education opportunities for pre- and in-service teachers:

- Recruited candidates for teacher education preparation;
- Provided technology training to in-service teachers;
- Provided student tutors to area schools;
- Increased the number of National Board Certified teachers; and
- Increased the percentage of teachers with advanced degrees.

One provision of the grant was to provide a four-year scholarship for OC Tech students to transfer after successful completion of the two-year Associate Degree to either Claflin University or SC State. Although these scholarships are available to all students, the recruitment of "other" race students which would transfer to our partner historically black institutions was emphasized. South Carolina Department of Education statistics (1999) show that with the minority public school student population in South Carolina of 42% and only 16% minority representation in the teaching force, therefore, the recruitment of minority teachers continues to be an important part of our mission and a critical challenge.

OC Tech has only scratched the surface of the potential of the college in preparing teachers. Currently, the college is working with surrounding school districts in meeting the requirements of the "No Child Left Behind Act" for paraprofessionals. The South Carolina Technical College System is partnering with the South Carolina Department of Education to provide a seamless system to carry paraprofessionals through the steps toward meeting better test requirements or educational requirements of this federal regulation. The Technical College System is also beginning a conversation with the South Carolina State Department of Education and the deans of four-year programs of teacher education to isolate areas for collaboration in providing opportunities for teacher education in the two-year institutions. The CHEC collaboration has provided a model that other entities in the state may wish to consider.

CHEC partners not only accept courses from the state-approved transfer block but also have extensive articulation agreements in teacher education which provide a "seamless pathway" for teachers in training. There is also a cross-registration program for students of the three institutions, allowing them cross-registration privileges at the institutions.

OC Tech has also participated as a leader in providing technology-based training for teachers in its region in partnership with the South Carolina State Department of Education. School districts use OC Tech's facilities and personnel for technology training. As a partner, OC Tech has access to software that is standards-based, that has been provided to school districts throughout the Title II grant.

Students and faculty from OC Tech have also worked in surrounding school districts and daycare facilities to provide instruction and tutoring. This venture gives our students opportunities to become familiar with the requirements of the teaching profession, as well as provide assistance to the citizenry.

Dealing with a shortage of 2.4 million teachers nationwide is a serious problem mandating innovative solutions. To overcome it will require the efforts of all participants in higher education. The CHEC partnership has shown the potential for two-year institutions to be an integral force in providing the nation with the highly-qualified teachers it must have to meet the needs of a domestic and international economy.

"Call Me Mister" Program

Dr. Tony J. Manson
Collaborator
Claflin University
Orangeburg, South Carolina
and
Mr. Ferrante Johnson
Graduate Assistant
Clemson University
Clemson, South Carolina

The teaching profession has changed drastically, perhaps much more than our society and changed demographics would suggest. Changed demographics have created student populations with very different family backgrounds to the extent that students in today's classrooms come from more diverse backgrounds and socio-cultural influences. Therefore, there is a pressing need for teacher preparation programs to attract wider audiences to the profession. South Carolina has a teacher recruitment and retention program targeted toward African-American males and their presence in elementary classroom. This is the "Call Me Mister" program, a U.S. Department of Education-funded program. University and college participants include Benedict College, Claflin University and Morris College; Clemson University is the lead institution and fiscal agent.

Introduction

Historically, mainstream teacher preparation programs have focused on educators and their efforts to work effectively with only one group, middle-class citizenry (Banks, 1994). However, the profession education has changed drastically, and it is necessary for teacher education programs to train prospective teachers for classroom diversity. Diversity has been defined in various different ways depending on region or location.

Too few teacher preparation programs have incorporated distinctly positive attitudes about minority group cultures or issues of ethnicity and race in their pre-service and in-service teacher training. It is not known yet that if a minority teachers' presence can change the present outcomes, but we should agree that some minority students view themselves as being isolated from others from an advantage socio-economic settings.

Ethnic Minorities and The Teaching Profession

The teaching profession has changed drastically perhaps much more so than our society and demographics would suggest. The demographic changes have created a student with a very different family background. The students we see in today's classrooms come from a more diverse background with many cultural differences. There is also a growing need for the teacher preparation programs to attract the minority ethnic and racial groups into the teaching profession, which could target urban areas. Students need to be able to identify with persons that look somewhat like them, which may be a reason why there are not many minority teacher educators seen by students (Manson, 1998).

There is extensive research on how students learn. Teachers who believe that the way to deal with culture or diversity issues is to individualize learning tasks are unlikely to create opportunities for pupils to learn from one another. Those who would like to view someone other than the majority race as teachers and teacher educators offend some. There is a continued outcry for ethnic minority teachers, but the minority population who attend our colleges and universities are continually choosing not to go into the teaching profession.

A teacher preparation program should do everything reasonably possible for students to experience early teacher-student classroom interaction (even confrontational ones). The program should recruit and develop as many minority educators as possible. Even though very little can be done regarding salaries or teaching conditions, the programs can sell teaching to the nation's outstanding high school students. Minorities on teaching faculties can greatly enhance teacher preparation programs. Minority students need to see persons in their images, as role models. The top minority students who believe they can be successful may be attracted to the teaching profession. They can become what are needed to reshape the next generation of learners (Boyer, J. B., & Baptiste, H. P. (1996). The visibility of minority educators can encourage retention among minority students. Experienced teachers at school sites can help sell their students on the teaching profession and show them how creative ideas are needed for career enhancement. Teachers need to be better educated and prepared for challenges they currently face in urban school districts. Of course, the recent violence in schools events does not help. The teaching profession must meet all the challenges ahead. The vision of a teacher preparation program has to approach these concerns with enthusiasm and vigor (Manson, 2002).

"Call Me Mister" Program

In South Carolina, there is a recruitment and retention program for African American males to become elementary classroom teachers. This is "Call Me Mister" program. The program is in its third year. The South Carolina universities that participate in it are HBCU's (Benedict College, Claflin University, and Morris College). There have been problem which occur in any program in its early stages, such as, finding the number of committed young men to fit into a position that is not very lucrative and time demanding. Another problem is the program require these young men pass the PRAXIS I examination by their sophomore year. This proves to be difficult due to the past history of African Americans on standardized exams. However, the program is out to dispel the notion that African Americans do not pass exams or matriculate at the university level with high proficiency.

Claflin University has had the distinct honor to host some of America's most watched daytime television shows. Mr. Jeff Davis, Field Director, and the "Call Me Mister" program received several awards during the 1st years of the program. Also, several interviews were given for television programs aired in South Carolina and nationwide. Television stations in Columbia and Spartanburg, S.C., highlighted the program in April of 2001. Among the highlights of the program since its existence are many articles in Black Issues in Higher Education, the USA Today and a segment in the Oregon State University Barometer news publications.

The Mister program have been involved in unforgettable events. Namely, presentations by the Honorable Alan Paige, the first African American to serve on the Minnesota Supreme Court and pro football Hall of Fame. In May of 2001, following the media attention generated by the Oprah Winfrey broadcast, Orangeburg City and Orangeburg County Councils presented public proclamations in separate, independent actions to the program for the positive influence, honor, distinction and public service generated by the program. The Mister gave an outstanding presentation to the State Legislature of South Carolina.

The term MISTER concept stands for the following:

*M*en
*I*nstructing
*S*tudents
*T*owards
*E*ffective
*R*ole Modeling

According to the statistics complied by the Executive Summary of Outcomes for the first two years of the Mister program some of the most important questions about the program and progress relating to recruiting, training, certifying and placing 200 African-American males in the public schools of South Carolina were answered. The following statistics were found:

- The ages of the students in the program range from 17 to 23

- The overall retention rate for students in the Call Me Mister Program (CMMP) is approximately 71%. This exceeds the retention rate for "regular" students on the three campuses (Benedict college, Claflin University, Morris College).
- The average GPA for students in the spring semester 2002 was 2.9. This average exceeds the average GPA of "regular" students on the three campuses.
- The Praxis I pass rate is up 40 percent on all three sections. In addition, 61.9 percent of students who have taken the Praxis I passed one or more sections.
- Students spent between 6 and 15 hours per week in activities related to their academic program for 2001-2002 compared to 7.76 hour per week for 2000-2001.
- When asked if the "Call Me Mister" program gave them a sense of purpose in their lives, 81.6 percent responded very favorably that it did.
- Over 75% of the Misters have indicated they plan to undertake graduate study for the master's degree after receiving teacher certification and entering the teaching profession.
- Most of the Misters (89.5 percent) believe they are being prepared for their professional roles as elementary teachers.

Preparation

The content of teachers usually consists of three major components: (1) liberal (or general) education, (2) specialized subject-field education, and, (3) professional education. A liberal arts program combines the arts and sciences and seeks to give prospective teachers board cultural backgrounds. The specialized subject-fields comprise a cluster of courses in specific subject areas and provide them an extensive preparation in their chosen teaching fields. Professional education consists of courses designed to provide knowledge and skills regarding the arts and science of teaching. It is important that perspective teachers explore what teachers do in the classroom (Baptiste, P. H., Baptiste, M. L. (1980). Teachers have to be able to teach and manage their classrooms effectively and efficiently. Teaching involves a complex series of acts. Teaching must fit the learner, the subject content, and the knowledge or the skills being taught.

Previously teaching was thought of as an art, but more recently it has moved in the direction of being a science due to the influences of research. There are a number of discernible things a teacher should have knowledge of to be successful. According to Boyer (1993), it is believed there are nine basic functions that teachers should be required to do. They are:

- The management of instruction
- The management of student behavior
- Instructional presentation
- Instructional monitoring of student performance
- Instructional feedback
- Facilitating instruction
- Communicating within the educational environment
- Having a firm knowledge of culture and diversity
- Performing non-instructional duties

These basic functions provide an overview of the major sets of knowledge and skills. Those planning to become a teacher should learn, practice and be able to perfect in order to become successful in teaching. The "Call Me Mister" program has a stated vision that embodies the thinking behind instituting such a program. The following is that vision:

"Call Me MISTER"

I am a young, strong African American male,
Dedicated to perpetuating a sorely needed concept...
Men as role models in elementary schools.
I am devoted to planting seeds of dignity and respect in children
and inspiring children to cultivate them and produce
a crop of unprecedented success.
I will teach reading, writing, and arithmetic and progress to
self-esteem, imagination and determination.
Because of my immeasurable promise
not only have I earned respect, I demand It!
A title is important only if one's character and
integrity dictate its use...
when you address me, please verbalize my destiny...
please don't call me by my first name...
call me in reference to my great vision...
Call Me MISTER!

References

Ashton, P., & Webb, R. (1986). *Making a difference: Teacher's sense of efficacy and student achievement.* New York: Longman.

Banks, J. A. (1994). *Multiethnic education: Theory and practice* (3rd ed.) Boston: Allyn and Bacon.

Baptiste, P. H., & Baptiste, M. L. (1980). *Multicultural teacher education: Preparing educators to provide educational equity.* Washington, D. C.: American Association of Colleges for Teacher Education.

Book, C., Byers, J., & Freeman, D. (1983). Student expectations and teacher education traditions with which we can and cannot live. *Journal of Teacher Education*, 34, 9-13.

Boyer, J. B., & Baptiste, H. P. (1996). *Transforming the curriculum for multicultural understandings: A practitioner's handbook* (p. 200). Caddo Gap Press.

Boyer, J. B. (1993). *Cross-racial instructional dynamics: Instructional interaction.* EDCIP- 9 10 Multicultural Programming, (November 4, 1993).

Brown v Board of Education (1), 347, U. S. 483, (1954).

Carnegie Task Force on Teaching as a Profession. (1986). *A nation prepared: Teachers for the 21st Century.* New York: Carnegie Forum on Education and the Economy.

Good, T. L., & Brophy, J. E. (1994). *Looking into classrooms* (6th ed.). New York: Harper Collins.

Grant, C. A., & Sleeter, C. E. (1989). *Turning on learning: Five approaches for multicultural teaching plans for race, class, gender, and disability.* Columbus, OH: Merrill-Prentice Hall.

Manson, T. J. (2002). *Teacher education preparation for diversity*, Lewiston, NY: Edwin Mellen.

Manson, T. J. (1998). *Cross ethnic, cross-racial dynamics of instruction.* (Eric Document Reproduction Service No. ED 429141).

Morrison, G. (2000). *Teaching in America (2nd ed.). Needham, Heights, MA: Allyn and Bacon.*

National Council for Accreditation for Teacher Education. (1995). *A vision of the future: The new professional teacher project.* (Brochure.) Washington, DC: Morrison, George.

Zehm, S. J., & Kottler, J. A. (1993). *On being a teacher: The human dimensions* (pp. 5-15). Newbury Park, CA: Corwin Press.

Families Adopting Wellness Needs (FAWN): A SCSU Program Educating Families About Wellness

(L - R) Dr. Ken Mosely, Dr. BerNadette L. Williams, Mrs. Myra Royal, Mr. Stephen Martin, (not appearing Ms. JoAnn Ward)

Dr. Ken Mosely, Professor & Chair
Department of Health & P.E.
and
Dr. BerNadette L. Williams
Assistant Professor
Department of Health and Physical Education

Families adopting Wellness Needs (FAWN) was a community based program designed to educate families about the benefits of proper exercise and nutrition. This program was initiated in the spring of 2001 with funding from the Community Higher Education Council (CHEC) and Local Education Agencies (LEAs) Program. The purpose of the program was to educate families about the needs and values of participating in lifestyle activities that promote wellness within the family unit. The objectives of the program were as follows: (1) to encourage participants to increase their involvement in physical activities; (2) to increase the knowledge base of each family in selecting, preparing and eating nutritious meals; and (3) to use wellness and exercise related activities to increase family time spent together. The family unit was considered an important element in promoting physical fitness, exercise, proper nutrition and wellness among individuals who do not regularly participate in organized wellness.

Families Adopting Wellness Needs (FAWN) was a community based program designed to educate families about the benefits of proper exercise and nutrition. This program was initiated in the spring of 2001 with funding from the Community Higher Education Council (CHEC) and Local Education Agencies Agencies (LEA's) Program. The purpose of the program was to educate families about the needs and values of participating in lifestyle activities that promote wellness within the family unit. The objectives of the program were as follows: (1) to encourage participants to increase their involvement in physical activities; (2) to increase the knowledge base of each family selecting, preparing and eating nutritious meals; and (3) to use wellness and exercise related activities to increase family time spent together. The family unit was considered an important element in promoting physical fitness, exercise, proper nutrition and wellness among individuals who do no regularly participate in organized wellness activities.

Since it has been found that far too many students have misconceptions or misinformation about fitness, the family unit was selected as the vehicle to re-educate individuals about the values of exercise and proper nutrition (Placek, J. and others 2001). Families Adopting Wellness Needs was also considered a very unique program because it involved the cooperation of several local partnering schools, the South Carolina District United States Tennis Association Southern Section and three local institutions of higher learning (South Carolina State University, Claflin University and Orangeburg-Calhoun Technical College) working together to promote wellness. The need to involve families in enjoyable educational experiences in exercise and nutrition education was very important in this program. It was believed that families who enjoyed their experiences would have a greater desire to continue these types of wellness activities after the program had ended. Everhart (1998) reported that innovative programs that incorporate physical fitness have been found to be more enjoyable than a traditional approach.

The FAWN program was considered an innovative program and it was structured to present wellness activities in an enjoyable and rewarding learning environment. The FAWN Program was organized so that participants and their families could participate in three different learning stations (tennis, aerobics and nutrition education) during six Saturday sessions. Each Saturday session began at 8:30 A.M. and ended at 1:30 P.M. The participants spent approximately 45 minutes at each station. Instructions was provided by a highly motivated staff which included four professionals and three college students (one each) from the partnering higher education institutions in (CHEC). The participants also received a nutritious meal during each program session and the family members in attendance were given an opportunity to participate in a recreational activity at the end of each Saturday program.

During the past two years the program has been considered a great success. More than two hundred individuals have participated and benefited from the FAWN Program wellness activities. With over 11 million of today's youth whose health is at-risk due to obesity (Everhart and others, 1999). The on-going challenge of the FAWN program and others like it is to increase the desire of families to participate in wellness experiences. Schools have recognized obesity as a problem among school age children, and they are on the front lines in helping to educate parents and their children about the ever-increasing health problems associated with obesity (Scanlon, 2003). The

FAWN Program believes that families can play a major roll in improving the wellness status of its members, and this program will continue to help educate people about the benefits of exercise and proper nutrition for developing healthier and happier family members.

References

Evenhart, B., Evenhart, L., Sands, C., & Dunnaway, D. (1998). The effects of combining a fitness emphasis during motor skill practice on third graders enjoyment of physical education lessons. *The Physical Educator*, 55, 114-120.

Evenhart, B. Brown, D. Harshaw, C. Gbroderick J., StubbleField, E., Williamson, B., & McDonough, R. (1999). The effects of a curricular fitness integration on the heart rater and skill improvement of elementary physical education students. *The Physical Educator*, 56, 91-97.

Gleaton, T. (2001). Tennis Anyone, U.S. Tennis Association joins efforts to revive local interest in sports, promotes wellness. *The Times and Democrat*, Orangeburg, S.C., Wednesday, February 28, 2001.

Gleaton, S. (2003). Fatty, fatty, two-by-four.... can't get in the weight room door. *The Times and Democrat*, Orangeburg, S.C., January 14, 2003.

Harrel J., McMurray, R. Gansky. S., & Bradley, C. (1999). A public health vs. a risk base intervention to improve cardiovascular health in elementary school children: The cardiovascular health in children study. *American Journal of Public Health*, 89, 1529-1535.

Hooper, C., Muuoz, K., Mac Connie, S., & Gruber, M. (1998). A family fitness program for children with learning disabilities in remote regions. *Rural Special Education Quarterly*, 17, 28-32.

Placek, J., Griffin, Dodds, P. Raymonds, C., Tremino, F., & Jamers A. (2001). Middle school students' conceptions of fitness: The long road to a healthy lifestyle. *Journal of Teaching in Physical Education*, 20, 314-323.

Scaulon, Bill. (2003). The big problem: Schools emphasize exercise to battle childhood obesity. *The Times and Democrat.* Orangeburg, S.C., January 7, 2003.

Teacher Quality Enhancement Partnership: Partners in Education. U.S. Tennis Association joins effort to revive local interest in sport, promotes wellness. *Partnership NEWS Letter*, South Carolina State University. Vol. 1, (2) Spring 2002 p. 9 &16.

Project PRIMER

Dr. Martha Jean Adams-Heggins
Professor, School of Education
and Project Director
South Carolina State University

The question in this article isn't whether HBCUs make a difference, but how HBCUs addressed the issue of nontraditional students as it related to Head Start reform. Dr. Martha Jean Adams-Heggins shares a program funded by the Administration on Children, Youth, and Families/Head Start Bureau from 1997 – 2002 designed to develop a model to train undergraduate and graduate Head Start personnel; and, lessons learned in the process of implementing the Project PRIMER model. Project PRIMER achievements include: a) approximately 270 participants that were officially admitted to undergraduate/graduate programs; that exceeded the recruitment goal by some one hundred individuals, and b) while the original grant was funded to serve 15 students, by its completion date of May 2002, had graduated approximately twice this number.

Head Start Partnership With Historically Black Colleges and Universities: South Carolina State University 1997 – 2002

"The Black College has a special calling...to reach the unreachable, to teach the unteachable, to embrace the rejected, and to be patient with the late bloomers."

---- Rev. Jesse L. Jackson

Introduction:

The White House Initiative on Historically Black Colleges and Universities (HBCUs) began with the signing of an Executive Order by President Jimmy Carter in 1980, and continued to gain momentum throughout the Reagan, Bush, Clinton, etc. Administrations. Perhaps, history will reveal that utilizing the capabilities of Historically Black Colleges and Universities (HBCUs) to improve the long-term effectiveness of Head Start and Early Head Start grantees, by developing models of academic training and forming partnerships between HBCUs and Head Start grantees and delegated agencies was truly one of the most ingenious ideas of the Administration on Children, Youth, and Families (ACYF) in the twentieth century. As many of you know,

HBCUs have a long and impressive history of success working with Head Start employees (nontraditional students).

In 1997, ACYF awarded financial assistance to eight (8) HBCUs. The purpose of these initial grants was two-fold. 1) to develop models for training Head Start personnel at the undergraduate/graduate levels; and 2) to graduate at least fifteen (15) Head Start employees by the end of the four-year funding cycle. Four-year grants in the amount of $500,000 ($125,000 per year) were awarded to Cheyney University, Howard University, Jackson State University, Kentucky State University, North Carolina Central University, Tennessee State University, Texas Southern University, and South Carolina State University (SCSU). Subsequently, Project Preschool Readiness Intervention Managing Education Resources (PRIMER) at SCSU was born.

Project PRIMER partnership/collaboration was composed of the following Head Start programs: 1) Aiken/Barnwell Regional Head Start; 2) Beaufort-Jasper EOC Head Start; 3) Carolina Community Action, Inc. Head Start; 4) GLEAMNS Human Resources Commissions, Inc.; 5) Lowcountry Community Action Agency, Inc.; 6) Orangeburg-Calhoun-Community Action Agency, Inc.; 7) Pee Dee Community Action Agency Head Start; and 8) Waccamaw EOC Head Start. It should be noted that these combined partnerships provided services and support to more than 7,500 rural, low income at-risk children and their families in the state of South Carolina.

During the first two years of the project (1997/98 - 1998/99), both undergraduate and graduate students were enrolled. But, during the last two years (1999/2000 - 2000/2002) only graduate students participated in Project PRIMER. As mentioned previously, this change was mandated beginning the 1999/2000 funding year to insure that the objective, i.e. to graduate a minimum of fifteen (15) students was met.

Goals and Objectives

The primary goal of Project PRIMER was to create a dynamic, high quality, professional development- training model for Head Start personnel. A subsidiary aim was to improve the quality of education and services provided to young children and families in Head Start programs in the State, Region, and Nation. The expected benefits of Project PRIMER were to: 1) Increase the number of bachelors/masters degree level Head Start personnel by 2003; and 2) Increase the pool of Head Start personnel who can serve as advocates for poor children, children with disabilities as well as for their parents. The Project's combined measurable objectives were:

1) to recruit 100 Head Start employees for the bachelor's degree program;
2) to recruit 60 Head Start employees for the masters degree programs;

3) to provide experiences culminating in either the bachelor's or masters degrees in the area of Early Childhood Education;
4) to provide relevant in-service staff development for Head Start workers to include teacher aides, bus drivers, and food service personnel.

The Model

The format for Project PRIMER's model has been primarily that of a weekend college. This arrangement made it possible for Head Start personnel to enroll, study, and maintain a full-time position while earning a degree. While following the curriculum set by the university, part of Project PRIMER's model was to seek "Best Practices in Early Childhood Education" using cognitive, affective, and psychomotor domain research and informed opinions to under gird the core of its pedagogy and enhance the University's program. Subsequently, students were also required to participate in intensive summer institutes to study the educational cutting edge topics of both Conflict Resolution and Mentoring. Additionally, based on both the School of Education's model and the National Board of Professional Teaching Standards, a great deal of emphasis was placed on the process of reflective teaching. To this end, activities that utilized this process were always included in all early childhood education courses.

Likewise, training, teaching techniques, and strategies follow principles known to enhance adult learners. Chief among these techniques are:

1) The relevance of the information,
2) The opportunity for participants to connect their own experiences with the new information, and
3) Time for application and evaluation (by implementing the new ideas in the actual work environment). Furthermore, in all courses in the discipline of early childhood education, assignments are divided into three major sections:

a. Theory (pedagogy essential for being a leader in the early childhood profession and for passing PRAXIS II Examination);

b. Field-based curriculum assignments (application in the work environment). For example, the assignment in ECE 514 - Early Childhood Methods & Materials provided students with a Mentor/Protégé Teacher. These placements were at the early childhood level (1st - 3rd grades in several school districts throughout the state during the regular summer programs. The students' final assignment at the site was the completion of a satisfactory micro-peer-teaching package. Included in this package, were the demonstration lesson plans, a video taped lesson demonstration, and evaluation from the mentor/protégé teacher, a peer teacher, and a self-reflection/evaluation.

c. Portfolio Assessment (connect one's experiences with new information throughout all courses in the graduate program). Additionally, portfolios are required for graduation.

Accomplishments and Achievements

Our achievements to date include approximately 270 participants who were officially admitted to the undergraduate/graduate degree programs. This number exceeded the recruitment objective by some one hundred individuals. Also, while the original grant was funded to graduate fifteen (15) students, Project PRIMER by its completion date of May 2002 graduated almost twice that number. The graduate students according to degree programs were:

- Eight (8) students completed the Master of Science in the area of Individual and Family Development (IFD). The eight IFD students were: a) Betty J. Hines, b) Charlotte P. Gamble, c) Berley James, d) Evelyn Patterson, e) Gloria Sarge, f) Geraldine T. Shaw, g) Ernestine W. Weisner, and h) Joyce H. Zaleski;
- Two (2) students completed the requirements for the Master of Education (M.Ed.), i.e. Vivian Henry and Anita Reaves-Legette;
- Twelve (12) students completed the Master in the Art of Teaching (MAT) program. The twelve students in the MAT program included: 1) LaMecisa Bethea; 2) Barbara Cooper, 3) Florrie Edwards, 4) Sharon Ellison, 5) Bertha Felder, 6) Elaine Fuller-Kennedy, 7) Elizabeth Greene, 8) Mollie Haynes, 9) Mary LeGrant, 10) Miriam Miller, 11) Peggy Murray-Davis, and 12) Helen Tomlin.

It should be pointed out that Project PRIMER students in the Masters in the Art of Teaching (MAT) program in the area of Early Childhood Education (ECE) at SCSU must also fulfill initial teacher certification requirements as part of their graduation requirements. Therefore, we are pleased to report that all 12 MAT (nontraditional) students passed the PRAXIS II on the first attempt with an average score of over 600. Historically, nontraditional students at this university have had little success obtaining passing scores on this standardized test.

We feel that there are two main reasons for this high level of success. First of all, the design and implementation of Project PRIMER's model considered strategies to meet the needs of its nontraditional students. To this end, students participated in several special classes and study sessions that were designed to provide and improve test taking as well as time management strategies. Secondly, a great deal of this success is due to the computerized assessment program (the Student Oriented Comprehensive Knowledge

Enhancement Technique Model) designed by Dr. Ashok Satpathy that was incorporated into classes such as ECE 513 - The Early Childhood Curriculum. Also to be considered in this success story is the positive attitudes and hard work ethics of Project PRIMER's students and staff.

The students in the Master of Education program were directed to write a thesis that would have a direct application for Head Start. As indicated previously, Vivian H. Henry and Anita Reaves-Leggette completed this requirement. Ms. Henry's thesis addresses Variance in Head Start Children's Academic Achievement According to Family Structure. This empirical study examined whether a child's academic growth is influenced by a household headed by a single parent or a household headed by two parents. It was found that academic achievement was not significantly influenced by family structure. According to Ms. Henry, there is a need for more research on the role family structure plays on the academic success of students in Head Start, especially in rural areas.

Ms. Reaves-Leggette's thesis was a Follow-Up of the Impact of Single Gender Child Development Classrooms on a Select Group of African-American Males in Project Head Start. This study followed up a selected group of African American males, to determine if Single Gender Child Development Classrooms in Head Start had any lasting effect on the males' performance through the 3rd grade. The results showed that these African-American males, in elementary schools, did just as well or in some cases better than their peers on statewide tests such as the CSAB, MAT 7, BSAP, and PACT. To this end, the data from this study indicated that single gender child development classrooms in Head Start do contribute to the academic success of African-American males in elementary schools. According to Ms. Reaves-Leggette, Head Start does work!

Students in the IFD program also contributed to the body of literature in Head Start/early childhood education/ and family studies by completing Problem in Lieu of Thesis on topics such as: a) Conflict Resolution in Daily Life; b) Building Self-Esteem in Children; c) Grief and Loss: The Road to Recovery; d) Child and Family Support in Head Start Programs; e) Parents in Control Successfully; e) Stress: Managing your Stress Or Else; f) The Seven Habits of Highly Effective Families and g) Male Parenting.

Finally, in conjunction with the collaboration between Project PRIMER staff and Region IV: Training and Technical Assistance Office Western Kentucky University, professional development opportunities were provided to several hundred other Head Start employees in the "partnership" through workshops, conferences, institutes, and community forums.

Reflections

There were three major concerns that we would like to share as a result of the lessons learned from this project. First, the major challenge for Project PRIMER was the lack of adequate funding, causing serious financial difficulties for both the project staff and students, especially during the fifth year. The grant for Project PRIMER officially expired September 30, 2001 and despite the request, no additional funds were approved by ACYF. However, additional funds were needed to support the remaining graduate students enrolled in the MAT program. It should be pointed out that the 12 students in the MAT program had completed all of the requirements for graduation except Student Teaching. To this end, funding and support for Project PRIMER's fifth and final year was provided by South Carolina State University in cooperation with Orangeburg Consolidated School #5. Therefore, Universities, Head Start partnerships, and funding agencies need to be cognizant of this situation as Head Start employees/students continue to enroll in various degree programs at South Carolina State University and throughout the nation.

Second, it is imperative that the quality of the early childhood degree program and the university's standards are not compromised. Yet, there will be special needs of nontraditional students that must be addressed. Part of the success of Project PRIMER has been the utilization of the knowledge that when working with nontraditional students, advisement, orientation, counseling, planning, and scheduling are critical aspects that must be implemented throughout the program.

Third, we have learned that the adult learners in programs such as Project PRIMER have unique academic, social, and emotional needs that require special support from the University, their Agencies, and their Families. Recognizing this, Project PRIMER made special efforts to address the unique affective needs of this group by providing personal guidance, tutoring, personal development workshops, seminars, and a great deal compassion. Therefore, Universities, Agencies, Families, etc need to take this matter into consideration as Head Start strive to meet the implementation of legislation, Section 648A, that by September 30, 2003...at least half of all Head Start teachers in center-based programs must have an associate, baccalaureate, or advanced degree in Early Childhood Education.

Mentors of New Teachers Need Training for Effective Mentoring

Dr. Clemmie F. Hill
Associate Professor
Department of Health and Physical Education
South Carolina State University

Mentors of new teachers must be required to participate in well-planned inservice workshops to develop skills for mentoring first-year teachers. First-year teachers must not be left to fend for themselves. In order to develop a pool of professional mentors who must have the necessary credentials, as well as, the expertise to train beginning teachers will necessitate the expertise of seasoned mentors. This preparation will enhance the mentors' ability to be a positive force of change; to have an understanding for what new teachers need to know; to be able to establish an effective mentoring relationship; to have a defined description of the role of the mentor, and to be a competent role model.

Mentors can have a significant impact on the professional development of first-year teachers. Whether a mentor's impact is positive or negative depends upon how well informed and skilled the mentor is. Effective mentoring depends on the mentor's commitment, knowledge, competence, skills, experience, and availability. Mentoring is a comprehensive effort directed toward helping a protégé or beginning teacher, develop the attitudes and behavior skills of self-reliance and accountability within a defined environment (Kay, 1990).

It has not been determined why, but in documented cases, school administrators have left first-year teachers on their own to sink or swim. However, former Secretary of Education Richard Riley, during his tenure, took a long look at the educational system in the United States and recognized there was a need to protect its investments. He suggested a planned program for mentoring first-year teachers. Dr. Riley encouraged those who have mentoring programs to make sure the mentors are carefully chosen and preparation should be provided. As mentors assist new teachers in reaching their goals and objectives, the mentors' professional skills continue to grow and to be enhanced. Organized preparation to become a mentor can only strengthen mentoring skills. Mentors who give their best efforts include those who have received formal preparation and have worked within their own discipline (*Christian Science Monitor*, 2000, June 27).

Mentoring by experienced teachers is a favored strategy in the United States (National Center for Research on Teacher Learning; (NCRTL). One would think that since selected mentors are the best a school district has to offer, all that would be needed is to assign an experienced teacher to a first-year teacher. The task of mentoring seems to be a relatively easy task. After all, the experienced teachers selected as mentors are considered by their peers and administrators to be master teachers. However, since education in general and children, content and the process of teaching, in particular, are constantly changing, what works well for one person may not be successful for another. Preparation would enhance and reinforce experienced teachers' good skills in the cognitive (knowledge), affective (relationship), and psychomotor (process) domains that are used in effective pedagogy.

Lipton, Wellman and the staff of the Association of Supervision and Curriculum Development (ASCD) studied the need for and the importance of mentoring new teachers in K-12 schools. This study culminated in a 2003 publication titled "Making Mentoring Work." The study emanated from the knowledge that today's high-pressured environments cause a lot of difficulty for veteran teachers. With beginning teachers, the pressure is greater in that they are entering the teaching profession armed with content knowledge, but situations may occur in the classroom that the college or university text books never cover. And very few tools for developing relationships with students, other teachers, parents, administrators and the community have been stressed.

Mentoring Template

Effective mentors should participate in on going mentoring preparation programs (Rowley, 1999). Changes in pedagogy and content are constantly made each year; therefore, staff development must involve preparing selected teachers to be mentors. Mentorship is a mixture of formal and informal learning, training and preparing experiential opportunities (Janas, 1996). One of the most important parts of the mentor program is the preparation for those who serve as mentors. Thies-Sprinthall (1986) and Hurst and Reding, (2002), suggested the following be included in a mentor or first year teachers' preparation program:

- Preparation in communication
- Listening skills
- Relationship skills
- Effective teaching skills
- Modeling of classroom management skills
- Coaching techniques
- Conflict resolution and problem solving skills

Training in Communication Skills

Communication is the key to effective mentoring. The communication skills of mentors are critical to the mentoring process. Communication occurs in different ways. Vocal communication is the most frequently used means of communication, but body language and writing are just as useful and effective. Mentors must be taught different methods of communicating. It must be impressed upon them that non-verbal communication is as effective and potent as verbal communication.

People communicate volumes through body language (Beth and Reding, 2002). Jotting down a note of encouragement is as important as writing out a list of things to do or correct. Body language, facial expression, gestures can assist mentors in understanding first year teachers' professional behavior, strengths and weaknesses. These aspects of the preparation program should provide ways of using verbal and non-verbal language in a supportive manner. Different methods of communicating should be explained, demonstrated and practiced.

Constructive criticism and methods of encouragement should be demonstrated and practiced. Prospective mentors should be provided communication scenarios to develop responses; opportunities to role play communication situations, and to discuss how they would handle mentor and novice teachers' communication venues. This is not to say that experienced teachers do not know how to communicate, but this added dimension of communicating provides them the opportunity to examine their communication skills and use them appropriately when working with the first-year teachers. Communication workshops help to build the self-confidence of mentors, thus strengthening their relationship skills.

Listening skills

Communication requires exemplary listening skills. It would be helpful if there were a college course in listening in that it is a necessary skill for all aspects of life. Often times listening is not used effectively. Listening is hearing what is not being said, as well as what is being said when talking with novice teachers (Janas, 1996). Mentors should be taught to listen with their eyes and their ears. Mentors must listen between the lines. Questions should be asked to make sure everyone understands what is being said.

Hearing the needs and interest in novice teachers' voices, and not responding at all may be just as important as responding positively to them. Many times, new teachers just need someone to listen to them; to be a sounding board (Boreen and Niday, 2000). After speaking their thoughts to the mentor, first year teachers come up with their own answers that fit the situation.

Other times they need input (Hurst and Reding, 2002). They need feedback from the mentor. Mentors must be good listeners in order to give constructive feedback.

Listening may seem like an automatic part of mentoring, but it may be one of the most difficult interpersonal skills to master. A formal course, for mentors should include the development of adept listening skills. Listening skills must be practiced for them to be fine-tuned, and mentor preparation should include planned sessions for mentors to work on listening skills.

Relationship Skills

A meaningful relationship between mentors and first year teachers is the heart of the supportive process (Freedman, 1993, White-Hood, 1993). Planned sessions should be designed to instruct mentors in ways of understanding the values and expectations of novice teachers. Behavior skills that demonstrate the need for respect and sensitivity to the needs of new teachers should be included in the preparation.

A program that emphasizes the acceptance of the mentor by the novice teacher is needed. Fundamental to any cooperative endeavor is empathy, accepting another person without making judgment; identifying with another (*Webster's New World College Dictionary, 1999*). The mentor learns to work with what new teachers bring with them. A mentor guides, instructs and shepherds. A mentoring-preparation program should suggest ways to nurture first-year teachers. Some educators refer to nurturing as shepherding, supporting or being advocates for a process.

Preparing mentors for nurturing or supporting beginning teachers includes: 1) learning to be the loudest advocate for first-year teachers; 2) standing beside the new teacher and sometimes in front as a shield; 3) helping with relationships involving peer teachers and personal relationships; 4) identifying and practicing ways to point out perceived errors made by novice teachers in a manner that the new teacher will not feel like a failure; 5) practicing saying what you mean and meaning what you say; and 6) examining ways of being consistent, patient and thoughtful.

A problem in developing relationships in which mentor-teachers need preparation is switching from working with children to working with adults. This is a totally different relationship. Most mentors are chosen because of their success with children (Fawcett, 1997). They know children's needs and provide direct instruction when necessary. This approach may not work well with first-year teachers who have been making decisions for themselves since they entered college. First-year teachers want desperately to prove that they know the answers. They want to appear capable. Therefore, mentors need help in switching from working with children to working with adults. No matter how great the teachers are in the classroom, mentor preparation in developing relationships is an essential prerequisite.

For mentors to strengthen their relationships with novice teachers, they must not be afraid to learn from the new teacher. They must be excited about what they are doing (Clark, 2001). The excitement rubs off on the new teachers. Relationship skills include being a good communicator which includes being a good listener. All the relationship skills mentioned will be relatively ineffective if communications skills are weak. Workshops that provide mentors' guidelines for establishing and maintaining cohesive relationships will assist everyone in aiding new teachers with their development of self-confident and trust. These two traits are needed to provide a stable beginning for new teachers.

Effective Teaching Skills

Successful mentoring is the ability to engage teachers in conversation about what effective teaching is about (Clark, 2001). Clark adds that support is needed to help new teachers refine what they can do to overcome obstacles related to planning, executing the plans, evaluating students' performances and contacting parents. Mentor preparation should emphasize skills in planning, presenting and evaluating. Mentors should be on one accord about the scope of what their role should be in guiding effective instruction. Mentors and novice teachers working together can identify the various instructional areas, when to provide assistance and how much assistance is needed. New teachers need models of good instruction, but being a good teacher does not mean one will automatically be a good mentor.

Directed teaching supervisors and those who would like to be cooperating teachers (the teachers that supervise or mentor the student teachers on the school site during the clinical experience) must be required to attend appropriate workshops. These workshops are designed to give the latest information on writing goals objectives, daily lesson plans, standards of evaluating and content teaching. The mentoring program, which bridges the gap between student teaching and the first-year of teaching, should be organized in such a manner that the mentors have the same kind of training before becoming mentors.

Preparation in mentoring gives mentors the opportunity to refine their instructional skills, gives the mentor tools of observation, works with diverse audiences, and crafts methods of designing and clarifying content. These methods would include presentation of content, skills of paraphrasing, summarizing, mirroring, and choosing challenging strategies. The mentor will demonstrate, in workshops, ways of interpreting, illustrating and demonstrating the characteristics of effective teaching to the first-year teacher.

Management Skills

To be an effective educational practitioner, it is necessary to establish a classroom in which learning is supported and allowed to take place (Graham, 2001). The first and most important skill to develop is being able to control the classroom in which one is in charge. Rink (1987) said establishing the learning environment has been called a first-base skill. You cannot get to home plate without getting on first base. Getting on first base is only the first step to scoring a run. Without establishing such an environment, there is little chance that learning will occur.

Mentor preparation prepares the mentors for guiding the new teacher in the classroom. Mentors are experienced teachers chosen because of their managerial and instructional skills. Preparation helps the mentor to identify how and when to assist the new teacher with his or her managerial skills. It will reinforce the new teacher's ability to suggest and model strategies for operating the class smoothly by using different ways to deal with inappropriate classroom behavior. Guiding new teachers into moving through all phases of the classroom management from setting up and distributing materials, to handling a student who is not paying attention, as well as to those disturbing the class with noise or unnecessary actions.

Managerial training as a part of the mentoring program will aid the mentors in verifying that the methods they are already using establish structures through which the class routine becomes predictable and operates smoothly. They may also introduce them to new strategies to establish structure. The mentor can learn ways to model or communicate managerial tasks to assist the novice teacher in establishing limitation for behavior and teacher's expectations for the students.

Preparing mentors for developing management tasks should reflect ways of establishing rules and expectations. Even though novice teachers come with some managerial skills, they will need assistance from mentors in some situations. New teachers will need to learn to provide laws for the classroom. They will also need to be guided in setting the tone of the general classroom atmosphere that will convey their beliefs about control and responsibility. How well mentors get this lesson over to novice teachers may determine the career longevity of new teachers.

Coaching

Coach is a term that is sometimes used interchangeably with the word mentor. A mentor is assigned to a new, capable and skilled, beginning teacher to provide examples, suggest activities and offer encouragement to the novice when there is a need. Coaches help new teachers to define their goals and to establish action planned strategies to reach them (Podsen & Denmark, 2000). The coach should be a trained observer, an encourager, willing to give a helping hand when the first year teacher seems to have failed in spite of following instructions. A coach is one who can give feedback to positive and negative procedures used by teachers.

Preparing to be mentors should include ways of identifying and recognizing the coaching and mentoring roles. Other coaching responsibilities that the preparation could aid would include: ways of developing respect for new teachers opinions; being verbally supportive of the new teacher; and being there for the new teacher at school and away from school. Coaching the new teacher requires strengthening the beginning teacher's attitude, content knowledge, and managerial and instructional skills.

Coaching is directed toward the new teacher and should be personalized to assist in identifying and clarifying the role of the new teacher in the educational system. Mentors need coaching guidelines that will allow them to identify their limitations in coaching, to place the timing of feedback, to encourage the new teacher to move forward, or reteach, and to know when to step back from the situation verbally and physically.

Conflict Resolution and Problem Solving

Holding children accountable for their behavior is one of the least enjoyable tasks of teaching, but one that all teachers must do to provide a conducive learning environment (Graham, 2001). Conflict resolution is a managerial task; however, it was given special emphasis because first-year teachers will need to know it goes beyond organizing the classroom. Conflicts will arise among students. Problems are a part of the daily lives of many students and many times the conflicts spill over into the schools.

Conflicts may occur in response to new teachers or other students. Mentors should have conflict resolution and problem solving workshops in order to give the new teacher recommendations, and strategies to help children solve their conflicts. Mentors need instruction in giving new teachers constructive ways of identifying problems before they get to violent confrontations (fighting). Mentors also need ways of solving problems of those who are involved in conflicts to pass on or reinforce the skills of the first-year teacher. They also need to know where to go to get help in solving the problems that are causing the conflict. Mentors need to help new teachers with parent conferences of children who are bullying or in constant conflict with other children. Learning how to recognize problems of the children in the classroom will be a valuable asset to the first-year teacher. Mentors must work with new teachers in pointing out problems without labeling the students.

Conclusion

School systems should foster the development of teacher-mentoring programs. The most important part of the mentoring program is a preparation program for prospective mentors. This preparation must be designed to cover all facets of working with the novice or first-year teacher. The length of the program may vary according to the needs of the prospective mentors. School systems today are finding that first-year teachers need much support to develop appropriately. Research indicates that mentoring will keep more first-year teachers from quitting (Scott and Piet van Lier, 2001). Therefore, it is important that beginning teachers get guidance regarding procedures, expectations and relationships. They need a link to other personnel; assistance with lesson or instructional plans based on district guidelines and pacing schedules (Valley View School District, 2000-2001), and a host of other things vital to their well being. A well-organized professional preparation program can effectively prepare mentors in efficient mentoring/supervisory roles.

References

Agnes, M. & Guralnik, D. (Eds). (1999), *Webster's New World College Dictionary.* (4th ed.). New York: Macmillan

Boreen, J. & Niday, D. (2000). Breaking through the isolation: Mentoring beginning teachers. *Journal of Adolescent & Adult Literacy.* 44, (2). 152-66.

Calvert, D. (May 2001). New teacher mentoring programs *Physical Therapy*, American Physical Therapy Association, Inc 81 (15) 58

Clark, F.T. (2001). The best practices of mentors. *Classroom Leadership Online.* 4 (8) Retrieved April 6, 2003 from http://www.ascd.org/readingroom/classlead/0105/1may01.html

Establishing Productive Mentoring Relationships. Retrieved April 6, 2003 from http://www.gse.uci.edu/Mentor Teacher/Chapter 3.1.html

Fawcett, G. (1997). Is a good teacher always a good mentor? MLRN's *"Mentor" Journal* 1 from http://www.mentors.net/for%20Journal1/J1.GtchrGmentor.html

Freedman, M. (1993) Fervor with. Infrastructure: Making the most of the mentoring movement. *Equity and Choice.* 9 (2), 21-26.

Graham, G., Holt E., Hale, S., & Parker, M. (2001). *Children Moving.* 5th ed. Mountain View CA: Mayfield Publishing Company

Hurst, B., & Reding, G. (2002) *Teachers Mentoring Teachers.* 493 Fastback. Bloomington, IN: The Phi Delta Kappa Educational Foundation

"Is training really necessary?" Retrieved April 6, 2003. from http://www.gse.uci.edu.MentorTeacher/Chapter4.html

Janas, M. (1996, Fall). Mentoring the mentor: A challenge for staff development. {Electronic version}. *Journal of Staff Development* 17, (4)

National Center for Research on Teacher learning. (n.d.). Retrieved March 21, 2003 from http://www.educ.msu.edu/alumni/newed/ne66c3~5.htm

Norton, J. (1999, fall). Teachers get help from the "guide on the side." *Reforming middle Schools & School Systems.* Retrieved April 6, 2003 from http://www.middleweb.com/CSLB6 guide.html

Podsen, I., & Denmark, V. (2000). Coaching and mentoring first-year and students teachers. (Eye on Education). Abstract retrieved April 12, 2003, from http://www.enc.org/resources/records/full/0%2C1240%2C025111%C00.shtm

Rink, J. (1987). The learning game: a baseball theory of teacher effectiveness. Unpublished manuscript.

Rowley, J. (1999,May). The good Mentor. *Educational Leadership.* 56 (8). Retrieved. April 6, 2003 from http://www.ascd.org/readingroom/edlead/9905/rowley.html

Scott, S., & Lier, P.V. (2001, Oct./Nov.). *Mentoring for first-year teacher is the law in 2002*: Will Cleveland be ready? Catalyst: For Cleveland schools.

http://www. catalyst-cleveland.org/10-01/1001story1.htm

The Christian Science Monitor (2000, June 27). A shift from 'sink or swim' to mentoring new teacher. Retrieved February 6, 2003 from

http://web1.infortrac.galegrou.../purl=rcl_GRCM_0_CJ62974148&dyn=71ar_frnt?sw_aep=mille

Thies-Sprinthall, L. (1986). A collaborative approach for mentor training: Q working model. *Journal of Teacher Education*, 37 (6), 13-20.

Valley View School District 365U (2000-2001). *Guidelines for first-year teacher program mentoring*. Romeoville & Bolingbrook. IL: Author White-Hood

Kay, R.S. (1990). Mentoring: Definition, principles, and application. In T.M. Bey & C.T. Holmes (Eds.) *Mentoring: Developing Successful New Teachers.* Reston, VA: Association of Teacher Educators.

Lipton, L., & Wellman, B. (2003). *Making mentoring work: An ASCD Action Tool.* Baltimore, MD: Association for Supervision and Curriculum Develpment.

GEAR UP: Helping to Make a Difference in Allendale School District

(L – R) Dr. Tony-Adams Aburimé, Paula Harris, Sandra Garcia

Tony-Adams Aburimé, Ed.D., Associate Professor Principal Investigator, Project GEAR UP South Carolina State University

Paula Harris, Ed.S., Superintendent, Allendale County School District

Sandra Garcia, B.S., Director SCSU Project GEAR UP

The SCSU GEAR UP program provides a variety of academic, social, cultural, and enrichment activities to seventh and eighth grade students at the Allendale-Fairfax Middle School in Allendale, South Carolina. It also provides activities for parents and training/staff development activities for the school's teachers and staff. Project activities are scheduled during both the academic year and the summer.

Project Overview

South Carolina State University Project GEAR UP (Gaining Early Awareness and Readiness for Undergraduate Programs) provides direct services to middle school students in the Allendale County School District to ensure that these children have the opportunity to achieve academically and are prepared for college. Two cohorts of approximately 260 students (130 seventh graders and 130 eighth graders) are now enrolled in GEAR UP and will continue through high school graduation. Direct services to the students include tutoring; mentoring; counseling; enrichment instruction; field trips (educational, cultural, and recreational); college visitations; college preparatory, financial aid and other related workshops. The project provides staff development activities to assist teachers and other school staff in identifying best practices for enhancing student achievement. Parent activities include family-school partnership training, college-planning workshops, and opportunities to serve as school volunteers and participate in other parent involvement activities.

Major Strategies

Both cohorts of students are currently receiving, through external consultants, motivational workshops designed to increase self-esteem, respect, responsibility, determination, and self-discipline. All consultants report excellent cooperation from GEAR UP participants. Additionally, students are receiving in-class tutoring in the areas of math, English/language arts, and science. The in-class tutoring and the after-school program are designed to increase the number of students who meet South Carolina State Performance Standards (perform at or above grade level on the Palmetto Achievement Challenge Tests-PACT).

Recent Activity Highlights

During the 2002-2003 school year participants in both cohorts traveled on luxury charter buses to Atlanta, GA. Many reported that this was their first trip out of South Carolina. While in Atlanta, students visited the Cable News Network Center, better known as the CNN Center and the World of Coca Cola Museum.

During the spring of 2003, students traveled to the campus of South Carolina State University to view a production by the University's Henderson-Davis Players entitled "Mufaro's Beautiful Daughters." Following the play students enjoyed pizza with the University's First Lady, Mrs. Frances "Ladybug" Finney.

In May 2003 both cohorts participated in a Family Night Celebration Banquet. At this event Mrs. Paula Harris presented students with "21st Century Scholars Certificates" signed by the U.S. Secretary of Education, Dr. Rod Paige.

Each summer students participate in a summer academic program and the "Annual Superintendent's Back-to-School Retreat." The 2003 summer program included two out-of-state field trips. The first trip was to Charlotte, NC, to the campus of the University of North Carolina-Chapel Hill and to Discovery Place, an interactive science center. To wrap up the summer program participants enjoyed a three-day trip to Florida to visit the Kennedy Space Center, the campus of the University of Florida and Universal Studios.

Current Outcomes

Teachers report an increase in positive in-class attitudes and behaviors as well as academic performance for project participants. A review of the most recent PACT scores for participants indicate an increase in student English/language arts scores (South Carolina State Department of Education, 2002). Since teachers reported that in-class tutoring seems to provide the best results for participants, we have increased the number of tutors in math, English/language arts and added tutors for science.

References

Aburimé, T. A. (2000). Gaining Early Awareness and Readiness for Undergraduate Programs (GEAR UP). Grant Proposal submitted to the U. S. Department Education. South Carolina State University, Orangeburg, S.C.

Allendale-Fairfax Middle School PACT Scores (2002). S. C. Department of Education, Columbia, S.C.

U. S. Department of Education, Office of Postsecondary Education (2002). GEAR UP: Current Project Overviews, Washington, DC.

Reaping What You Sow: Mentoring Beginning Teachers

Ms. Geneal G. Cantrell
Teacher in Residence
Furman University

My first year was in a self-contained setting. My mentor was not a good role model. She had different views on the purpose of a teacher in special education. From my experience, my mentor did not have enough time to be a mentor because of her own responsibilities. My first year was a hard one. (Anonymous reflection of a first-year teacher)

Year after year an eager crop of new teachers arrives at the doors of our nation's schools. Many are fresh out of their teacher preparation programs. For the most part, they are excited, enthusiastic, and possess the feeling of being able to conquer the world. They are primed and ready to motivate, inspire, and teach the students in their charge. These teachers enter the profession (as many of us do) to make a difference in the lives of children. It is exciting to see these young novice teachers enter the teaching profession, yet frustrating to watch as they face the stark realities of today's ever challenging classrooms. Novice teachers are often assigned to teach the most challenging students and with the least resources. Today's teachers must be better equipped to respond to increasing student diversity in the classroom, significant family and social issues that affect student learning, lack of adequate funding for education, and public mistrust of those responsible for educating our future citizens.

Teaching is the only profession in which entry-level individuals are expected to perform from day one exactly like their experienced counterparts. It is also one of the few professions that lack a universal, formal structure for entry into the profession. Most professions require a residency, internship, apprenticeship, or other formal training experience. Teaching requires none of these during the first year of teaching. In education we regularly place our first-year teachers, our "rookies," into the starting lineup of the "game." Far too often they strike out. In other professions this "striking out" is expected and often accepted, but not so in education. First-year teachers are expected to perform at the same level of expertise as their veteran counterparts.

One of the toughest challenges facing our public schools is not only attracting enough qualified teachers to fill our teaching vacancies but also retaining them once they are employed. The South Carolina Center for Teacher Recruitment, in tandem with the South Carolina State Department of Education, report 12.2 % of new teachers leave after the first year of teaching with as many as 33.3% exiting the profession after five years (Payne, 2001). South Carolina's statistics for retention of novice teachers are comparable to those in other states. With fewer people selecting education as a viable career choice and an increasing number of teachers approaching retirement, these figures are just not acceptable. We are betting the future of this country and the dreams of our children on our nation's teachers. How will that future look if we continue to lose teachers to other professions? What does the system need to do to better prepare and retain these novice teachers for the "trench warfare" that is all too often occurring in the classroom?

Literature Review

The Southeast Center for Teacher Quality located at the University of North Carolina in Chapel Hill, North Carolina conducts research and informs policy in order to enhance opportunities for all students to have competent, caring, and qualified teachers. A policy brief, The Status of Teaching in the Southeast: Measuring Progress, Moving Forward (2003), states that the teacher turnover problem in the Southeast is severe and only getting worse. This trend must change if we, as a society and an educational system, are going to "leave no child behind." The National Center for Education Statistics (2000) reports that teachers who do not receive any type of induction support or mentoring during their first year leave the profession at a rate almost 70% higher than those who receive it. It appears that the key to the retention of teachers in the profession is a top-quality mentoring program that provides the guidance, encouragement, and support new teachers need to get them through the difficult early years. Most experts will agree that investing early in the development and growth of new teachers is a strategy that pays off in the long run. When new teachers have the necessary guidance and support from master teachers during their first year of teaching, they tend to stay longer and adjust better.

Barnett Berry, director of the Southeast Center for Teacher Quality, conducted a workshop (March 12, 2003) for the South Carolina Center for Teacher Recruitment that was titled Getting Serious About New Teacher Induction and Mentoring. The presentation was aimed at the Accomplished Teacher Network, a distinguished group comprised of South Carolina school district teachers of the year and other invited educators who have interests and opportunities to train mentors or serve as mentors for induction teachers. Berry's presentation informed the group of some of the most successful induction and mentoring programs throughout the United States. In his work he found common characteristics among the programs. The commonalities were: new teachers were not given the most challenging students, new teachers were given a reduced teaching load until they could pass or demonstrate competency in teaching, and new teachers were assigned well-trained mentors. These mentors were given released time to work with novice teachers as well as compensation and extensive, on-going training in mentoring. One additional commonality among successful mentoring programs was the requirement of universities to follow and support new graduates for two years.

John Goodlad (1998), renowned educator and proponent of school renewal, uses the analogy of comparing schools to gardens. He believes that teachers are to schools as gardeners are to gardens. He deems teachers as tenders not only of the plants but also of the soil in which they grow. What a telling statement! With teachers exiting the profession in growing numbers, increasing populations of students entering our schools, and impending teacher retirements, the question must be asked, how can we afford not to mentor new teachers? If educators do not begin to take care of their "gardens," then the results may be a continuing increase in the shortage of teachers entering the profession and those exiting the profession too soon. If we do nothing to change the soil to render it capable of nurturing and supporting our young tender plants (our novice teachers), then we may indeed reap what we sow.

Furman University's Teacher to Teacher Model

In 1997 Furman University, a small private liberal arts college in the Southeast, received a grant entitled "Recreating Colleges of Teacher Education," one of eight grants given by the BellSouth Foundation. This, coupled with the teacher education department seeking initial accreditation by the National Council for Accreditation of Teacher Education (NCATE), and affiliation with National Network for Education Renewal (NNER), led them to look for innovative and practical solutions to improving K-8 teacher preparation. After examining the results of a self-study comprised of exit evaluations from teacher candidates and alumni surveys, the university faculty began to explore ideas to transform the teacher education program (Crockett, Cantrell, Ritter, & Svec, 2003).

Andrew (1990) and Andrew and Schwab (1993) provided the university with the empirical evidence they needed to move forward and make the final decision with regard to the direction of a new teacher preparation program. A study based on a ten-year comparison of four- and five-year graduates of the teacher education program at the University of New Hampshire determined that five-year graduates exhibit a higher rate of entry into the teaching profession and remain in teaching longer than four-year graduates, as well as demonstrating greater competence of knowledge of a variety of teaching models, teaching strategies, classroom management, adapting curriculum for individual differences, and development of a philosophy of education (Andrew, 1990). Graduates of extended programs self-reported feelings of greater confidence as a teacher (Andrew & Schwab, 1993). In addition, graduates of extended programs have, as part of their preparation program, opportunities to engage in action research, more extensive practical experience before teaching, more confidence and competence, more opportunity to take additional coursework before and after the full-time internship, and have greater subject area expertise (Andrew, 1990).

Furman University took the first steps in the creation of a similar model by partnering with local school districts. Through this partnership both parties agree to commit to preparing teachers through a rigorous introduction to the profession, which includes field-based experiences with diverse student populations and deliberate experiences that connect theory to practice and content knowledge to methodology. The district/university partners believe that children will ultimately benefit if teacher candidates work closely with experienced teachers (mentors) and faculty who model exemplary teaching practices (Quast, 2003). Research shows that the most effective induction programs do more than just get novice teachers through the first year (Britton, Raizen, Paine, & Huntley, 2000).

Backed by theory and best practice, the university and local school districts worked collaboratively to design and create the Teacher to Teacher program. The model employs the notion of mentoring as one of its cornerstones serving to underpin and function as a strong foundation. Teacher to Teacher offers unique and substantive mentoring and support to first-year teachers. In this model, each participating district releases a mentor teacher of all teaching responsibilities to be a full time member of the Teacher to Teacher T.E.A.M. (Teacher, Encourager, Advisor, and Mentor). As a T.E.A.M. member the mentor will work with three to five first-year teachers in the program. Along with the released mentor, the university supervisor visits the induction teacher throughout the school year on a regular basis. The university supervisor no longer functions as just an evaluator of induction teachers. Instead the university supervisors serve as colleagues working together, side-by-side to improve teaching, encourage teacher leadership both in and out of the classroom, and model best practices, all of which result not only in greater teacher competence and confidence, but more importantly in student achievement.

Another member of the Teacher to Teacher T.E.A.M. is the Teacher in Residence, released from one of the participating districts. The Teacher in

Residence provides the communication link between the district, school administrators, teachers, and university faculty by providing a sounding board for concerns, fears, and questions. The Teacher in Residence also offers input and assistance in developing and implementing this budding program while also teaching classes to Teacher to Teacher participants during their Senior Block and the induction year, and also coordinating and conducting the training of mentors.

All members of the Teacher to Teacher T.E.A.M. come together twice a month for meetings to inform and update each other of the progress and needs of the first-year teachers for whom they are responsible. T.E.A.M. members are also required to dialogue through weekly reflections. Communication has proven to be a critical key to the success of the program. Collaboratively, the T.E.A.M. works to seek avenues to increase teacher effectiveness and encourage the growth and development of each induction teacher's journey to becoming a competent, confident, and caring educator.

Description of Inquiry Project

The Teacher to Teacher program began with a pilot group of ten students in the 1999-2000 school year. The second year (2001-2002), 21 students participated in the program, while 13 students are currently in their induction year in the classroom (2002-2003). The purpose of this inquiry project is to compare teacher perceptions as to the effectiveness of the mentoring received and its program components and overall satisfaction of the first year of teaching. The comparison groups were those teachers who matriculated through Furman University's Teacher to Teacher program and a corresponding sample of induction teachers who completed other teacher preparation programs. In addition to examining perceptions of induction teachers, this inquiry project also looked at the perceptions of the mentors. Data was gathered from mentor teachers to determine their perception of the effectiveness of the mentor training they received prior to the mentoring event, the support of the university during the induction year, and the implications of the experience as it relates to their own professional development. The majority of the participants in this project currently teach in Anderson and Spartanburg counties in South Carolina.

The instrument used for responses from these two groups was a survey developed by the researcher. It was designed to measure the perceived feelings of teachers regarding the mentoring they received during the induction year of teaching. A Likert scale, ranging from one to five was used to rate the items in the survey spanning from five "strongly agree" to one, "strongly disagree." Further, an open-ended question was asked at the end of the survey to glean other impressions and input from the participants.

The second portion of this inquiry involved mentors of induction teachers. The mentors were divided into corresponding groups. Group one consisted of those who served as a mentor to the induction teachers in the Furman Unversity Teacher to Teacher program and was comprised of seven participants. The second group of mentors was comprised of 27 teachers who served as mentors of induction teachers who completed teacher education programs other than the Furman University's Teacher to Teacher program. All of the participants in both groups currently serve as teachers in Anderson School District One or Spartanburg School District Six. For this group a set of interview questions was developed and administered by the researcher.

Inquiry Analysis and Findings

The findings of this project will be discussed in narrative form analyzing the significant areas of the surveys, as well as, the responses of the induction teachers and the interview responses of the mentors. With regard to the survey perceptions of the induction teachers and their responses to the questions, a number of areas appeared as statistically significant between the induction teachers prepared and mentored in the Furman Unversity Teacher to Teacher program and the other induction teachers questioned.

The area of strongest significance was that of "university support." The question posed was, "My college/university worked with my mentor during my first year of teaching." The responses to this question produced the greatest diversity between the means (4.7200 for the Teacher to Teacher participants and 1.5294 for non-Furman teachers). This strong indication of difference between the groups illuminates one of the major, most visible differences between the Teacher to Teacher program and other pre-service teacher preparation programs. Induction teachers in the Teacher to Teacher model receive support throughout the first year of teaching not only from their mentor teacher but also from a university supervisor and the Teacher in Residence. This scaffolding approach to mentoring enables the induction teacher to benefit from multiple perspectives and practical experiences from many angles.

The other areas of significance will be reported individually but organized within a thematic structure. These themes include time issues between the mentor/mentee, personal/emotional aspects of mentee perceptions of the mentor/mentee relationship, technical aspects of the classroom/mentor roles, and the overall perceptions of the efficacy of the mentoring process.

A first-year teacher in the Teacher to Teacher program shares her thoughts on how the program helped her during her first year:

> *I feel like I owe a great deal of my success as a first-year teacher to the Teacher to Teacher program. My mentor was an incredible support system for me. She provided a wealth of knowledge from all of her experiences. My teacher in residence was supportive as well. I especially found her helpful through the first-year teacher class she taught. My professor provided me with wonderful feedback, as she visited my classroom and kept up with my first year. Overall, I was incredibly blessed to have the team of people that I did to help me through my first year. I feel like I had an advantage over other first-year teachers at my school not participating in the program.*

The words of this teacher demonstrate the first emerging theme of this inquiry study, which was university support of novice teachers. This reflection serves as a powerful example of the unique and comprehensive support, mentoring, and nurturing of Furman University's Teacher to Teacher program. This induction teacher recognizes and appreciates the members of the Teacher to Teacher T.E.A.M. and credits much of her success during her first year of teaching due to her participation in Furman's extended fifth-year program. The true aim of everyone who aspires to be a teacher should be, not to impart his own opinions, but to kindle minds. Traditionally mentors have been thought of as "experts" who simply pass on all their "tricks of the trade" to novice teachers. Mentors in the Teacher to Teacher program are encouraged not just to wear the "expert hats" but to aspire to live up to and model Homer's use of the word mentor from The Odyssey, which was guide or advisor.

The heart of the Teacher to Teacher program is based on the premise of meaningful mentoring which best occurs through regular and ongoing reflection: reflection on your teaching practices, reflection about student learning, and reflection about teacher effectiveness. Throughout the first year of teaching, induction teachers are required to write reflections about their progress reflect on each student's diverse needs, their academic progress, and to share their own unique discoveries about themselves as budding educators. These reflections are shared with university supervisors and the Teacher in Residence, each of which in turn writes reflective comments. Meaningful reflecting occurs when university faculty respond to these reflections by sharing thoughts about past observations of the induction teacher, offering encouraging thoughts about accomplishments, and often, by posing philosophical questions for the induction teachers to ponder and explore in an attempt to foster further growth. As professional educators, university supervisors can provide invaluable support to not only the beginning teacher but also to the mentor teachers.

The National Center for Research on Teacher Learning (2003) is a web-based project that is supported in part by major grants from the Office of Educational Research and Improvement, US Department of Education. A brochure, Learning from Mentors: A Study Update, focuses on mentoring practices and the contributions of mentor teachers to novice teachers and their ability to teach. The study is still underway with data analysis ongoing. One of the initial findings of the study was that mentor teachers need time to mentor and opportunities to learn to mentor. In particular, mentor teachers need to: (1) critically examine their beliefs about teaching and learning to teach; (2) connect their practice as mentors to novices' learning; and (3) discuss dilemmas and problems that arise in the course of helping novice teachers learn to teach. As indicated earlier, mentor teachers in the Teacher to Teacher program have the opportunity to practice all three suggestions identified from NCRTL. They feel the support of the T.E.A.M. is critical to their individual abilities to teach, encourage, advise, and mentor.

The simple secret of this program is all too clear. It is this: it's all about relationships, mentor to mentee, university supervisor to induction teacher–one-on-one. The chance of T.E.A.M members being able to lend a helping hand through those difficult first lessons, to offer a listening ear when a parent conference didn't go as well as planned, and to cultivate and foster competence and confidence lends itself to retaining teachers in the profession.

A second emerging theme from the induction survey was the issue of time–time to spend with the mentee, time to discuss instructional issues, and the perception that the mentor had the necessary time to work with the induction teacher. A powerful developing notion from the non-Furman mentor teacher interviews was also that of time. Comments such as these were prevalent throughout the non-Furman interviews: "Having the time to mentor was my greatest challenge," "If I were to mentor again I would try to be more available, time restraints are very frustrating," "I suggest the district find a way to give the mentor teacher the released time needed to observe and mentor new teachers," and "Dealing with the lack of common planning time was a constant problem." One non-Furman mentor explained the dilemma of time as follows:

> *The greatest challenge I face as a mentor is having the time to mentor properly. While I'm required to do a certain number of observations as well as being there when my mentee needs assistance, I've been given no time to do these things. I'm still required to do my own full time job! That means I just have to fit things in when I can which is very difficult to do. Unfortunately something has to give when all this pressure is placed on me; often the one who suffers is the teacher I am mentoring.*

The most common problem in mentoring relationships is a lack of time for collegial conversations (Boreen, 2000). In the business world, new employees are usually given fewer responsibilities, but in education, the opposite is true. No differentiation is made for a 20-year veteran and a novice teacher. They are assigned an identical number of courses to teach and are expected to perform an equal complement of duties and responsibilities. The same is true in that no differentiation is made for the mentor teachers to have time to work with their mentees. Most mentors are expected to mentor on top of all of their other duties as a veteran teacher. T., who has served as a mentor teacher in the Teacher to Teacher program for two years, addressed this issue:

> *I do not know how any program can call itself a mentoring program without allowing time for its mentors to interact with the mentees. I have mentored first-year teachers before while trying to manage my own classroom/life and I look back and CRINGE! How unfair to give these first-year teachers false hope. It is impossible to give a regular classroom teacher one-tenth enough time to do a first-year teacher justice unless that person has numerous hours of released time.*

Mentors in the Teacher to Teacher program are given the gift of time. Paying attention to the needs and concerns of their mentees over the period of a full academic year creates a developmental perspective, rather than an episodic one. Time affords the opportunities to consult, collaborate and coach, thereby developing the novice teacher's capacity to generate his/her own learning and moving her or him toward competency and confidence in their classrooms.

Personal and emotional aspects of perceptions of the mentor/mentee relationship emerge as a third significant area of difference between the two groups surveyed in this inquiry study. Issues in this emerging theme include feeling comfortable discussing and sharing concerns with the mentor, relating to the mentor on a personal level, the mentor listens and accepts the mentee's ideas, and feeling respected the my mentor. It is important for mentors to create and construct a safe environment, where both verbal and nonverbal communication implies full attention and high expectations. In an emotionally safe environment first-year teachers will openly share concerns, ask questions, and accept constructive criticism. Emotional support can come in the form of a shoulder to cry on, a hug rewarding success when dealing with a difficult student, a listening ear, or responding empathetically to the new teacher's frustrations and short comings.

A key factor to the success of any mentoring relationship is mutual trust. Without the mutual respect and trust on both sides of any relationship, it will be doomed from the very beginning. It is hard for new teachers to openly share their shortcomings or weaknesses. However, trying and difficult events occur for all first-year teachers. C. describes the importance of her relationship with the Teacher to Teacher T.E.A.M. after one such event:

> *We had our meeting Wednesday [two university faculty and mentor] and I remember thinking how truly lucky I was. No one was pointing fingers at me or blaming me, everyone was there to help me! Everyone kept telling me that they knew I had the ability to be a good teacher but I just needed help getting there. I was so touched at all of the support and encouragement everyone offered. We arranged to have a meeting every Wednesday to discuss how the week had been going. [Professor], [professor], and [mentor] would ALL be visiting on a more regular basis and would evaluate my teaching in different areas.*

All of these wonderful teachers spent so much of their own time to help me. I really don't think that I could have made it through without each of them. I don't think there are enough words to truly express how grateful I am. I mean, I could have been "left behind" or forgotten. All I know is that I truly believe that Furman's education department is the best teacher program I have ever come across.

Teachers who leave the profession often site lack of support, feelings of isolation, and difficult working conditions as reasons why they left. With the guidance and support of the T.E.A.M., C. was able to successfully complete her first year of teaching. Her voice and comments about the Teacher to Teacher program provide evidence of the positive outcome of emotional support and mentoring.

Technical aspects of mentoring and mentoring roles surfaced as the next pattern in this inquiry study. Included in this pattern were ideas such as: I viewed my mentor as more of an evaluator, my mentor helped me with classroom management issues, and my mentor modeled lessons for me. Despite the many benefits of a mentoring relationship during the first year of teaching, it is important to note that tension can, and often does, occur during the first year of teaching between the mentor and the mentee. Tension can surface in a mentoring relationship due to a lack of time for assistance and help, philosophical differences between the mentor and the novice teacher, inappropriate length of the relationship, and failure to separate mentoring from evaluation (Lipton & Wellman, 2001). Mentors are not and should not function as evaluators. Requiring mentors to evaluate often creates a conflict between the involvement required for nurturing and the objectivity required for judging.

The National Commission on Teacher and America's Future (2003) studied Rochester's Career in Teaching (CIT), Albuquerque's Resident Teacher Program (RTP), and the New Teacher Project (NTP) of Santa Cruz, California, all of which are recognized as successful mentoring and induction programs. Included in these findings was the fact that all three programs contain extensive mentor training prior to the mentoring process and all meet throughout the school year on a regular basis. This time together affords mentors the opportunities to grow and learn from one another. Mentors in the Teacher to Teacher model also participate in training and many enroll in the Best Practices in Mentoring three-hour graduate course offered by the university, at no cost to the mentor.

The final theme, which emerged as significant between the two groups, was overall perception of the mentoring process. In Barnett Berry's presentation, Getting Serious About New Teacher Induction and Mentoring (2003), he shared that only 42% of teachers surveyed who began teaching after 1995-1996 reported that their mentors were helpful to a great extent during the first year of teaching. One hundred percent of the graduates in the Teacher to Teacher program said that the mentor helped them to have a positive first year of teaching (agree or strongly agree). This is best illustrated with the words of a Furman induction teacher:

> The mentoring program is an extremely beneficial program. It is so nice and helpful to have someone you can depend on for advice, specific help, and a shoulder to cry on. It is hard to help others when you have a classroom of your own, but a mentor with flexibility can aid you with challenging issues or just check on you. I KNOW that my mentor helped to make my first year a good one.

Currently 80% of the first graduates of the Teacher to Teacher program are in their third year of teaching. These same teachers all plan to return next year for their fourth year in the profession. Ninety percent of the second class of graduates will soon complete their second year of teaching. The two students who chose to not teach after their first year are currently seeking teaching positions for next year. One has applied and received a job to return to the same district in South Carolina where she completed her first year of teaching while the other is seeking a teaching position near her home. The third class of graduates is just finishing their first year of teaching and 100% plan to return for the second year. The researcher must note that the program is still in the infancy stage. Most reports and statistics on teacher retention report results after five years of teaching. Luckily the participants in the program remain in close contact with the university making it a simple task to continue to collect, gather, and analyze data about the success of the program.

The quantitative results of this study have demonstrated statistical significance as to the effects of quality, intensive mentoring. However, these results alone do not tell the impact of the effect of mentoring of this caliber. The voices and insightful reflections of both the Furman induction teachers and mentors provide the reader with the beliefs and personal day-to-day accounts of the power and influence of mentoring. S. recounts her experience with the Teacher to Teacher program:

> I am sending this e-mail to express my appreciation to Furman and the district concerning the Teacher to Teacher program. I cannot begin to express how integral my mentor teacher has been to my success this first year. I do not think it is possible to understand how valuable a mentor teacher is unless you are a first year teacher. The education majors from the year ahead of me told me countless stories of how critical their mentor teacher was to their teaching.
>
> One of the greatest contributions my mentor has been able to provide is how well she knows my kids. She has spent sufficient time in my room that she knows all the problems and accomplishments of each student. So, when I run into a problem with one of the kids, or a parent, or am in need of advice she can give me PRECISE and PRACTICAL help. Because my mentor is available to be in my classroom she is also able to model lessons for me, sit in on parent conferences, help me to plan lessons that fit my student's needs, provide remedial help to those students that I may not be able to give all that they need, and she can occasionally take over my class so that I can observe other teachers. All of these things would not be possible if I did not have a mentor like the one the Teacher to Teacher program provides. I am so grateful that I was able to have an opportunity like this.

S's heartfelt comments about the Teacher to Teacher model testify to the foundation of the program—teacher-to-teacher, a one-on-one relationship where mentor teachers support induction teachers through sincere, caring relationships working towards nurturing and growing new teachers.

Conclusions

This inquiry concludes with a strong affirmation of the Teacher to Teacher program. The researcher acknowledges the small number of respondents on the induction teacher survey but quickly asserts that the populations studied represent the entire teaching force of the Teacher to Teacher program as well as a corresponding sample of teachers of traditional teacher preparation programs who completed their induction year in the same districts studied.

> *The National Commission on Teaching and America's Future, No Dream Denied (2003), has identified six dimensions of quality teacher programs. The fourth dimension is entry-level teaching support in residencies and mentored induction. Teachers are not "finished products" when they complete a teacher preparation program. Strong residency and mentored induction experiences during their initial years in the classroom provide beginning teachers with invaluable support as they lay the groundwork to become accomplished teachers. A well planned, systematic induction*

program for new teachers is vital to maximize their chances of being successful in any school setting.

Clearly, the evidence of this inquiry indicates that the efficacy of the Teacher to Teacher program surpasses that of the perceptions of the traditional programs. The researcher believes that the components of this program constitute the basis of a collaborative partnership between a university teacher preparation program and local school districts to meet the demanding needs of the induction teacher of today. While the commitment of the university, as well as the school district is extensive, the results of the initial effectiveness and subsequent teacher retention of the inductees offset these efforts. The researcher believes if novice teachers can make the transition to the teaching world as smooth and gently as possible and achieve confidence quicker, they will more likely experience a genuine passion for the profession and be willing to remain in the profession longer than their peers. Teachers leave the profession for numerous reasons, many of which fall into the category of "is it really all worth it?" Teaching is not an easy profession, but it certainly is worth it. Most teachers enter the profession because they love children and have a strong desire to "make a difference in the lives of children." Teachers who have participated in Furman University's Teacher to Teacher program are not only remaining in the profession; many are emerging as leaders in their schools. It appears that indeed, we (Furman University's Teacher to Teacher T.E.A.M.) may be reaping what we sow.

Geneal Cantrell is a Teacher in Residence at Furman University in Greenville, South Carolina. She can be reached at geneal.cantrell@furman.edu

References

Andrew, M. (1990). The differences between graduates of four-year and five-year teacher preparation programs. Journal of Teacher Education, 41 (2): 45-51.

Andrew, M., & Schwab, R. (1993). An outcome assessment of graduates of eleven teacher education programs. Paper presented at the Annual Meeting of the American Educational Research Association, Atlanta, Georgia.

Berry, B. (March 12, 2003). Getting serious about new teacher induction and mentoring. Presentation to the Accomplished Teacher Network Mentoring Conference sponsored by the South Carolina Center for Teacher Recruitment. Columbia, South Carolina.

Berry, B., Luczak, J., & Norton, J. (2003). The status of teaching in the southeast: Measuring progress, moving forward. Southeast Center for Teaching Quality Policy Brief: University of North Carolina, Chapel Hill, North Carolina.

Boreen, J., Johnson, M., Niday, D., & Potts, J. (2000). *Mentoring beginning teachers: Guiding, reflecting, coaching.* Portland: Stenhouse.

Crockett, D., Cantrell, G., Ritter, S., & Svec, M. (2003). Collaborative efforts to retain new teachers: A university-school district partnership. Science Teacher Retention Mentoring and Renewal. Arlington, Virginia: National Science Teacher Association.

Goodlad, J. (1998). Ecology of School Renewal. Chicago: University of Chicago Press.

Lipton, L. & Wellman, B. (2001). *Mentoring matters: A practical guide to learning-focused relationships*: Sherman, Connecticut: Miravia.

National Center for Education Statistics (NCES). (2000). Progress through the teacher pipeline: 1992-93 college graduates and elementary/secondary teaching as of 1997. Washington, D.C. : US Department of Education.

National Center for Research on Teacher Learning. (2003, [May 12, 2003]). Learning from mentors: A study update. Available: www.ncrtl.msu.edu

National Commission on Teaching and America's Future. (2003). *No dream denied: A pledge to America's children.* Washington, D.C.

National Commission on Teaching and America's Future. (Summer, 2000). District induction programs that work. Urban Initiative Partners Newsletter.

Payne, L. (2001). Retention. South Carolina Center for Teacher Recruitment Newsletter. Columbia, South Carolina.

Quast, L. (2003). Teacher to Teacher: A model for a collaboratively supported induction year: Place of promising practice. Paper presented at the National Professional Development Conference, Orlando, Florida.

Concluding Perspective

Dr. Constantine W. Curris
President
American Association of
State Colleges & Universities
Washington, D.C.

The highly decentralized character of public education in the United States works against reform measures that are centrally mandated; yet, in schools and communities across America, educational innovation and improvement are commonplace. The readings in this monograph are testament to the vitality of the educational enterprise.

The crucial role of teacher education programs to the improvement of student learning is widely acknowledged. Yet, we are keenly aware that educational reform will not occur unless there is a systemic alignment of policies, practices and programs which impact public schools. A few examples illustrate this point. The most effective physical science preparation programs are of little value if there are no students pursuing these programs; the best prepared middle school teachers will not improve learning if middle school credentialing permits poorly prepared or excess elementary and secondary school personnel to teach in middle schools. The need and desire for teacher-specific and school-specific professional development and continuing education go for naught if colleges are locked into graduate coursework and schedules developed a half-century ago and irrelevant to today's teachers. Systemic chan

Partnerships are probably the most important mechanism to facilitate this alignment. Coordinated, coherent action will be necessary to achieve improved learning and to insure that the 'leave no child behind' concept moves from rhetoric to reality.

However, education remains at the mercy of public opinion. Two major obstacles remain to our nation's achieving the needed degree and expanse of reform. The first is the long-delayed adaptation of public education to the market economy. The thorny problem of insufficient numbers of highly qualified teachers in high demand fields such as mathematic, physics, and special education will be solved only when compensation is attuned to market conditions rather than fixed schedules. Simply stated, the glaring shortage of mathematics teachers will not be solved until their compensation approaches private sector salaries for mathematically talented graduates. Colleges and universities are in tune with the market; K-12 education is not.

Likewise, the maldistribution of teachers--with critical shortages far more prevalent in rural areas and inner cities--will not be addressed until higher compensation is provided by low-demand schools. In the private sector, employers provide higher salaries and bonuses for employees who work in remote and challenging places. Even the Armed Services provide additional compensation for servicemembers stationed overseas. We do the opposite in public education. The highest salaries and benefits accrue to educators in the most desirable settings--inexcusably penalizing students in rural areas and inner cities.

The second major obstacle is the public's reluctance to embrace teachers as professionals and to accord them the status of professionals. But we should not limit this reluctance to the "public" per se. We educators are equally guilty. Colleges and universities often view teachers as recipients of services rather than educational partners. Within the academy professional development for educators engenders different attitudes and priorities than similar programs for physicians, attorneys and virtually all other professions. While the literature of business overflows with testaments to staff training and on-going continuing education, professional development for teachers is rarely addressed, much less funded. Even teachers themselves deprecate their status and some discourage their students from pursuing careers in education.

Part of the challenge facing teacher educators is enhancing the worth of teachers and promoting greater self-esteem among practitioners. The movement toward establishing and enhancing partnerships is one of the most promising developments in education. Reducing structural barriers and personal misunderstandings, building collaborative efforts to align policy, practices and programs, and enhancing the value of a teaching profession are crucial to achieving the excellence for which we all strive.